BAPTIST PARTNERSHIP IN EUROPE

BAPTIST PARTNERSHIP IN EUROPE

J. D. Hughey

BROADMAN PRESS
Nashville, Tennessee

Dewey Decimal Classification: 266.4
Subject Headings: MISSIONS—EUROPE // BAPTISTS—EUROPE
Library of Congress Catalog Card Number: 81-66559
Printed in the United States of America

Preface

The main point made in my book *Europe—A Mission Field?* (Convention Press, 1972) is that, contrary to common opinion, Europe is a challenging arena for Christian missions. This fact still needs emphasizing. That is one reason for this book.

Of perhaps even greater importance than the "why" of missions in Europe is the "how"—and this is more a matter of attitudes and spirit than of methods. Missionary endeavors in Europe (and, indeed, in the whole world) must be on the basis of genuine partnership.

For thirty-five years I had the privilege of living and working in Europe as a partner of European Baptists and Southern Baptists. My wife and I spent the last four months preceding my retirement (at the end of 1981) with our missionary and national partners in Europe and the Middle East. Some of the nationals were former students of mine in Spain or Switzerland, and, in a few cases, both. With many colleagues, I had anguished over problems in churches, conventions, and institutions. With many there had been times of rejoicing over problems solved and victories won.

During our final tour, as my wife and I were welcomed and bidden Godspeed, we had the deep satisfaction of knowing that we were among friends and fellow workers whom we respected and loved and who respected and loved us. We heard and talked much about partnership in the gospel.

Soon after I became seriously ill early in 1982, I received

from the First Baptist Church of Madrid a letter with about one hundred and fifty signatures. My friends and partners in the gospel there wanted to assure me of their love, appreciation, and prayer support. The first Spanish Baptist service I ever attended was held in that church. Some of the best correspondence course and seminary students I ever taught were members of the church, and a former student is now its pastor. On my recommendation, the Foreign Mission Board helped the church to purchase property. The pastors and members of the church encouraged me in my attempts to preach in Spanish. They forgave my blunders. They helped me to identify with the Spanish people. They inspired and challenged me by their Christian faithfulness, their consistent stewardship, and their effective witnessing. They provided leadership for the Spanish Baptist Union and helped to create a climate in which partnership flourished.

The letter from Madrid included the following sentences: "We remember you with deep affection and appreciate all the efforts you made for the work here. The Lord used you as you collaborated so effectively. Our development as Christians and as a church is always associated in our thinking with Brother Hughey."

My development as a Christian and as a missionary is closely related to the people who wrote that letter and to many others like them. Do you wonder why I believe so strongly in Christian partnership?

This book is a revision and updating of *Europe—a Mission Field?*, with special focus on partnership.

To Mrs. Rebecca Sisk, my faithful and efficient secretary from 1964 to 1975, I am indebted for typing the manuscript.

Contents

1/Why Baptist Missions in Europe?

Is Europe a mission field? Is it a mission field for Americans? Even the question is offensive to some Europeans. Most Americans are willing to admit that Europe is a mission field, but many deny that it is as important a mission field as Africa, Asia, or even Latin America.

If missionary effort should be limited to uncivilized, uneducated people, non-Europeans would be very presumptuous to think of missions in Europe. If missions included only pagan people or those to whom Christianity is unknown, Europe would not be a mission field.

Europe is a mission field—first of all for European Christians and secondly for those willing to help them— because most people in Europe are not Christians in a personal, vital sense. A mission field is any part of the world, regardless of its background or history, where there are large numbers of people with spiritual needs that are not being adequately met in the name of Christ. Europe is such a place; America is also.

Jesus said, "The field is the world" (Matt. 13:38). The distinction between Christian and non-Christian countries has broken down. The whole world is a mission field. We Christians are sent into the world with the good news of Jesus Christ. American Christians have a special responsibility for fellow Americans, and German Christians for fellow Germans; but American Christians are also responsible for Germans, and German Christians for Americans. We need to join hearts and hands with each other.

9

Highly Developed Culture

"The workmen on that building did not go to school very much, but they are not ignorant men. They have absorbed much of the history, knowledge, and culture of the land." The speaker was a Spanish Baptist pastor. His words, addressed to a new missionary, were true. Even uneducated Europeans share in a rich cultural heritage. Beautiful buildings and great works of art surround them. They hear lovely music regularly and may sing arias while they work.

Of course, the level of cultural appreciation among the better-educated people is higher than among the un-schooled. The continent of Europe appreciates education. Most Europeans go to school. Although liberal arts colleges are virtually unknown on the Continent, and university education is not intended for everybody, many Europeans have now, and have had for centuries, the advantages of higher education. Universities were flourishing in Europe before America was discovered. It is an honor to be addressed in German as Herr Doktor and a still greater honor to be spoken to as Herr Professor.

The opera house is a prominent building in most European cities, and it is usually well filled for performances. Even while Vienna was almost prostrate after World War II, superb operas were being presented there. "But," you may say, "when I was in Europe last summer, opera houses were closed!" True. Tourist season in most places is not opera season, for many of the opera lovers are away on vacation and many tourists seek lighter entertainment.

Americans do visit Europe's great architectural monuments and artistic treasures. The Parthenon in Athens, the Coliseum and Roman Forum, the cathedral of Notre Dame in Paris, the cathedral of Cologne, the palace of Ferdinand and Isabella in Segovia, Michelangelo's statue of *David* in Florence, Leonardo da Vinci's *Mona Lisa* in Paris, Velazquez's *las Meninas* in Madrid, and the new suspension bridge in Lisbon—all of these speak of the ancient and still living culture of Europe.

What of literature? English literature is a significant part of the world's cultural heritage and is a staple of American education. Less well known than English writers, but no less important, are Dante, Goethe, Cervantes, Tolstoy, Victor Hugo, and many other European authors. The fiction of Europe is read everywhere. Philosophies produced in Europe (for example, Communism and existentialism) affect the whole world.

Europeans and Americans of European origin have been in the vanguard of scientific development. Science is one of the outstanding features of Western civilization. It has changed and is changing occupations, recreation, outlooks on life, and patterns of living around the world.

Christian Influence

Christianity has been a major influence in the development of European culture. The most imposing buildings in most cities are cathedrals and churches. Many villages are built around churches. Village life through the centuries has centered on the church. The greatest art has been religious. Much of the music of Europe reflects the Christian character of the continent. The Christian heritage is evident in literature. European laws also reveal Christian influence.

In spite of geographical and linguistic barriers, there is a certain cultural unity in Europe. What is it? Of course, the legacy of classical Greece and Rome has been passed on in greater or lesser degree to all of the countries of Europe, but more important than this is the common Christian heritage. Christianity has had much to do with making Europe "European."

The apostle Paul heeded a call to Europe: "Come over

into Macedonia, and help us" (Acts 16:9). Into the centers of European culture he went—Philippi, Athens, Corinth. Displaced Asiatics (Jews) and also Europeans (Greeks and Romans) believed Paul's testimony that God was in Christ reconciling the world unto himself. Communities of Christian disciples began to appear in Europe. Growth was rapid, for the church members were "lay preachers," ready to share the gospel with individuals and groups.

One of Paul's great ambitions was to preach the gospel in Rome, the main center of life in Europe and in the Mediterranean world. When at last he arrived in Rome, as a prisoner, some Christians who had preceded him to Rome went down the Appian Way to meet him. Whether or not Paul ever got to Spain, as he wished, is unknown. But we can be reasonably sure that before his death Christianity was established there, also.

Persecutions were severe, but imprisonment, beating, and execution could not stamp out Christianity. When a Christian was killed, frequently two arose to take his place. Within three centuries, most of the Roman Empire had been Christianized.

The Emperor Constantine perceived the vitality and power of the Christian religion. He reported that just before a major battle near Rome in the year 312 he had a vision of a cross of light in the heavens bearing the inscription, "By this sign, conquer." He conquered. Toleration and then favor were granted to Christians. Although he did not forbid the old religions, he limited them and granted royal favor to Christianity. It became easier to be a Christian than not to be one. Church buildings were built at royal expense. In order to define Christian belief, the emperor convoked a general church council and, though he was not yet baptized, took a prominent part in it. Later emperors made Christianity the official religion of the empire; they persecuted heretics.

Under such circumstances, most people in the Roman Empire became "Christians." Many were devout, but others were Christians of convenience. Church ritual and ecclesiastical power tended to obscure the gospel message and the New Testament ideal of the fellowship of believers. Still, European life and thought bore the seal of Christianity.

Even when the Roman Empire fell, the church continued. It kept the lamp of civilization burning in Europe. Many tribes became Christian under the influence of monks and nuns whose faith and culture were accepted as superior. Some remarkable "mass conversions" took place. For example, at the end of the fifth century the Franks followed their king, Clovis, in baptism. Russia became Christian in the tenth century when Vladimir accepted for himself and his people the Byzantine form of Christianity, developed in Constantinople.

Europe of the Middle Ages was "Christian." This was an age of faith—some of it genuine and some quite superstitious. Union of church and state prevailed, and religious dissent was dealt with harshly. Thousands perished in the Inquisition.

Christendom was threatened by the rise and spread of Islam. Palestine, North Africa, the Iberian Peninsula, southern Italy, and finally Constantinople, in 1453, fell to Muslim conquerors. The Muslim onward march was stopped only at the gates of Vienna, and not until 1492 were the Moors driven out of Spain. Some Europeans became Muslims. Pockets of them still exist on the continent. However, the conviction was strengthened that Christianity was the right religion for Europeans. Unfortunately, European Christianity had departed considerably from New Testament Christianity.

By the sixteenth century the church in western Europe was ripe for reform. The Protestant Reformation divided it. Some countries became Protestant, and others remained

Catholic. Europe still was "Christian"—though less united than before on what being Christian meant. Almost everyone was a member of the dominant church of his part of the continent.

Obviously, all Europeans were not Christians, not even all who said they were. Europe has never been a truly Christian continent, nor has any other. Church membership was almost universal; it still is in some countries. But many people had no personal Christian faith, and their conduct was as unchristian as that of persons who had never heard of Christ.

Although Christianity greatly influenced European life and culture, there was a flow in the other direction also. Customs and practices were regarded as Christian simply because they were characteristic of Christendom.

Baptists

The Baptist movement arose among people who believed that church members should be true Christians in faith and in conduct. The organized movement started in England in the early seventeenth century and spread to the European continent two hundred years later. Since then, Baptists have established themselves in almost all of the countries of Europe. The only exceptions are Albania, Luxembourg, and a few small countries such as Andorra. By 1981 there were 1,074,117 Baptists in Europe—more than on any other continent except North America and Asia. Baptists are few in numbers in most countries, but almost everywhere there is capable leadership.

In some European countries the Baptist movement was indigenous from the beginning. Obviously, this is true in England where Baptists started, but it is true elsewhere, also. In some places foreign assistance was given on a limited scale. Especially noteworthy has been the help provided in central and northern Europe by Baptists of the northern part of the United States. However, the number of missionaries was always small, and leadership was provided by Europeans.

In 1870 Southern Baptists sent missionaries to Italy, where they have had much to do with the development of the Baptist movement. Fifty years later further responsibilities in Europe were accepted. In an epoch-making conference of Baptist leaders in London in 1920, Southern Baptists were asked to continue their relationship to Italy, to take up new responsibilities in Hungary, Rumania, Yugoslavia, and parts of Russia, and to assume the responsibilities previously borne by Northern and Swedish Baptists in Spain. Northern Baptists (now called American Baptists) were to continue their assistance to Baptists of northern and central Europe. Other Baptist groups received more limited assignments.

A new stage in Southern Baptist involvement in Europe began after World War II. In 1948 a Baptist World Alliance conference in London decided to end the "mandate system" that had prevailed since 1920 and to leave each Baptist body in Europe free to receive aid from any other group in the Baptist World Alliance as might be agreed upon by all involved. By the end of January, 1982, 163 Southern Baptist missionaries were assigned to twelve countries of Europe. Financial assistance was given during the year for Baptist projects in several other European countries.

European Baptists not only receive foreign missionaries; they send them. With about six hundred missionaries serving overseas, the ratio of missionaries to church members is far better than that of Southern Baptists.

Growing Secularism

European Christians are painfully aware that their part of the world is losing its Christian character. Christianity is not a vital factor in the thinking and living of the majority of Europe's more than a half billion people. There are even references to our times as the post-Christian era. Jesuit theologian Karl Rahner of Germany said: "We live in a land of heathens, a land with a Christian past and certain Christian leftovers."

Secularization has gone far in Europe. This is not bad if by secularization we mean attention to this world, though not exclusively so, and the freeing of society from ecclesiastical domination. The loss of control by churches of governments and society is not bad. The erosion of Christian conviction and influence, which has reached flood proportions, is deplorable. Irreligion and secularism have swept across Europe. This is obvious in Communist countries, where the official philosophy is materialistic. It is less obvious but no less serious in the Western world, where materialism is just as pervasive, though not usually stated in philosophical terms. Even in lands where churches have become established, multitudes of people deny the existence of God or act as though he did not exist.

Until 1952 it was exceedingly difficult for a Swede to avoid or renounce membership in the established Lutheran Church. Even after the law was changed, few Swedes bothered to get out of the state church. Yet, though 97 or 98 percent of the people are Lutherans, only 5 percent attend church regularly. Several years ago Archbishop Brilioth said: "It is uncertain if today one would call Sweden a Christian country. The Christian clothing it wears is an illusion."

On January 5, 1970, *Newsweek* quoted a church official in Germany as saying: "Church membership has always been considered a necessary part of a man's standing in the community. As a result, our churches have just about the same public, institutionalized character as the municipal garbage collection."

This may be changing. On January 25, 1970, a popular

illustrated magazine in Germany, *Stern,* gave over five pages to a report on "The Break with the Church: Why Catholics and Protestants in Masses are Leaving the Church." The magazine stated that in Germany it is no longer a shame to drop church membership; on the contrary, it is becoming quite modern. Some say the church is irrelevant, that it does too little about injustice and evil in the world. Some reject Christian teachings. Others condemn the church because it countenances any kind of belief or disbelief in its members. Many Catholics protest against their Church's attempted restrictions on their freedom in such things as birth control. Many want to escape the "Church tax" imposed on those listed as members. One can be an atheist and remain in the Church; but if he does not pay his Church tax, he must leave the Church.

In a country where church membership is automatically begun in infancy through baptism, the number of purely nominal members is likely to be large. In every country where there is a state church, multitudes of people come in contact with the church only at baptism, marriage, and death—for "hatching, matching, and dispatching," as some have said. A similar situation prevails in countries where the tie between church and state has been broken but churches continue to be "people's churches," including a large part of the population in their membership on the basis of infant baptism. Church statistics from Catholic countries like Italy, Portugal, or Spain, where almost all of the people are said to be Catholics, or from Protestant countries like Sweden, Norway, or Denmark, should not blind us to the religious indifference and unbelief in those lands. Surveys have shown that 56 percent of Norwegians regard themselves as positive toward the Christian faith, but only 14 percent answered "yes" when asked, "Do you consider yourself a personal Christian?" and 8 percent said they were negative toward Christianity.

On October 1, 1979, *Newsweek* carried an article on the Roman Catholic Church in Europe with the title, "A Church in Decay." One piece of evidence submitted was the decline of the Society of Jesus, founded by Europeans four centuries ago. Today the majority of Jesuits are from India and the Americas. A Jesuit in Paris is quoted as saying, "We Europeans are a cultural minority within our own order. In 1960, there were 40 of us enrolled in my seminary class. Half have since left the Society—and the priesthood. Out of the 1961 class of seminarians, only one remains today."

The *Newsweek* article ends as follows: "Already, many parts of Europe are virtually mission territories where foreign-born priests say Mass in churches that are centuries old. It may take the faithful many more years to realize what is happening, but the signs are clear; the center of Catholicism may lie in Rome, but it can no longer draw on Western Europe for strength."

The picture is not altogether dark. A 1981 comprehensive international survey by the European Values Study Group, supported by private foundations, the European Economic Community, the Spanish Government, and the Roman Catholic Church, revealed interest in religion and the church. Spaniards, French, Italians, and Germans listed the church first when asked to indicate degrees of confidence in ten institutions, including parliaments, civil service, trade unions, and the press. The British put the police first and the church fourth. However, 76 percent of them declared that they believed in God.

Spiritual awakening in Europe is a real possibility. Some people are ready for it; others are not. Even the irreligion and secularism of our times may prepare the way for new religious experience.

European churches are trying in traditional and innovative ways to minister to people who may or may not seek such ministry. Some attempts succeed and others fail.

One must probably list among the noble failures the Autonomous Youth Center in Zurich, Switzerland, which was set up by the city, with financial assistance provided by churches and private organizations, after a series of noisy and even destructive youth demonstrations in sedate, conservative Zurich. Young people organized groups to operate two restaurants, a bar, a movie theater, and a printing press and to help runaways or young people with drug-related problems. For several months the Youth Center seemed to work well, but gradually it became a hangout for alcoholics, drug addicts, drug pushers, prostitutes, and pimps. Most of the idealistic organizers became disillusioned and left. As this is being written, city funds for the Center are frozen, and a rightist political party has taken one of the contributing churches to court. The needs of rebellious young people have been highlighted, but the search for ways to meet the needs goes on.

The Role of Baptists

Are Baptists ready for the challenge of times such as these? Baptists emphasize the personal and voluntary character of true religion. They believe in salvation by the grace of God through personal faith in Jesus Christ. They emphasize the baptism of Christian believers only and church membership limited to believers. They have not had embarrassing ties with governments. They are in strategic places throughout Europe. Will European Baptists accept the European continent as their mission field—not their only one, but the one of special significance for them? Yes.

At a European Baptist Conference in 1964 Jannes Reiling of Holland said: "There is no longer a Christian Europe. A new Europe has arisen—a worldly minded, godless, unchristian Europe which has set itself free of the Christian church and of God. . . . The West is developing

into an unchristian world; the East is openly anti-Christian
. . . Europe, whether East or West, is in fact a part of the
world that has turned away from God and the Christian religion."

At a conference of European Baptists in 1969 Ronald
Goulding, secretary of the European Baptist Federation,
said: "Europe has become a mission field in a sense which
no one would have been able to imagine before the First
World War."

The evangelism committee of the European Baptist
Federation, in a statement issued by its chairman, Gunter
Wieske, in 1970 said that Europe for the second time in
history has become a mission field, where perhaps less than
5 percent of the population are committed Christians. There
are signs that the church—"the only institution in the world
that can give men what they need, Christ"—is undergoing
renewal in various countries of Europe, but there are too
many church members "who have never been asked to
share what they have received." Wieske said a many-sided
modern evangelistic thrust is urgently needed.

Remarkable progress in developing the "many-sided
evangelistic thrust" has been made. One senses a growing
concern for evangelism throughout Europe, east and west.
Some details will be given in later chapters.

In a report on a 1981 Evangelism and Education Conference in Ruschlikon, Wieske mentioned widespread involvement in personal evangelism, new interest in principles
and programs of church growth, and international cooperation in evangelism.

In October, 1981, the Methodist magazine, *New World
Outlook,* indirectly recognized the opportunity and responsibility of Baptists by quoting the Lutheran German theologian, Jürgen Moltmann as saying: "The baptism of children
is the foundation stone of the state churches in Europe . . .
(There) is no possibility of creating a voluntary, confessing,

independent community out of institutional churches to which people belong simply on the basis of having been baptized as children."

Europe is, indeed, a mission field for European Baptists. They know it and are acting accordingly.

For Baptists, as well as for other Christians, the following words from Sir Kenneth Grubb, a European observer of the world Christian scene, are pertinent:

> I do not altogether despair of the Church and its mission in the world. I do not think that, at least in the West, we have yet discovered that approach to the presentation of the Gospel which makes it attractive, intelligent and convincing to modern man. I do not think that the customary arrangements of Christian worship fit very readily into the pattern of life of a sophisticated and industrial society, and I think therefore that a considerable adaptation in the life of the churches has to be made as a prelude to the reconstruction of religion as a living force. I welcome, therefore, with equal respect and gratitude, the great crusades carried on by Dr. Graham and the discussion group where the two or three meet and pray. It may well be that the words "revival" or "renewal" mean something far different from any of our conceptions today.

The Role of Southern Baptists

What can Southern Baptists do? They can help. When Europeans speak of Europe as a mission field, they sometimes add "*our* mission field." They do not think an invasion by American evangelists or missionaries would do the job. However, they know that the job is too big for them alone, and they graciously accept help that is graciously given.

There are fewer missionaries in Europe than in South America, Africa, or Asia, and the ratio is likely to continue. Some Southern Baptist missionaries are needed and are welcome in Europe. Large numbers would not be welcome in most countries and may not be needed. Southern Baptists did not start Baptist work in Europe. They have never been in charge of Baptist work in most countries, are not in charge of it anywhere now, and will never be in charge of it. In Europe, probably more than in any other continent other than North America, Baptist work is indigenous, with foreigners in a helping role. This is the trend everywhere. Europe may offer a preview of what is going to be the practice worldwide.

In a paper prepared for a 1982 consultation at Ventnor, New Jersey, on the role of North Americans in the future of the mission enterprise, David M. Stowe said:

> It is agreed that primary responsibility for mission in each place rests with the local or nearby Christian communities, but that missionary partnership in persons and funds can be immensely helpful if local partners set the terms of reference.

Funds and personnel provided should never rob Baptists anywhere of their right to set the terms of reference.

Sending missionaries is important. However, foreign missions is more than the sending of missionaries. Foreign missions advances God's kingdom in every way possible, including the strengthening of indigenous churches and institutions. Helping other people to do what ought to be done is as praiseworthy as doing it oneself.

I propose for Southern Baptists the following statement of purpose with reference to Europe: To help Baptists in Europe to share the Christian gospel in such a way that people of all backgrounds will accept Christ as personal Savior and Lord; to help develop vital, evangelistic churches; and to help demonstrate the relevance of Christianity to individual lives and society.

Southern Baptists can help to keep—or make—Europe Christian, or at least make known to some Europeans the saving grace and power of God.

2/The How of Baptist Missions in Europe

European Christians regard their continent as a mission field. Whose? Theirs, primarily. However, they recognize that need and responsibility are not contained within national or continental boundaries.

Europe is a mission field for Baptists, including Southern Baptists. How should Southern Baptists and European Baptists be related to each other? How can they best work together?

Partnership

Partnership is a key word in missions. The word suggests that different people are so related to each other and to a common enterprise that each has a part in it. A partnership is a close, cooperative relationship. Nations can be partners or allies. Business and professional people often establish partnerships.

The apostle Paul, an Asiatic, wrote to the first church established in Europe about partnership in the gospel: "I thank my God in all my remembrance of you, always in every prayer of mine for you all making my prayer with joy, thankful for your partnership in the gospel from the first day until now" (Phil. 1:3-5, RSV).

The Greek word Paul used is *koinonia*. When the focus is on the relationship of human beings to God, the word is often translated "communion." When the emphasis is on human relationships, the translation is usually "fellowship" or "partnership." In every case, there is a close, cooperative relationship.

Christians in a local church are partners in the gospel. So are those in a denominational body such as a state Baptist convention or the Southern Baptist Convention. Christians of different countries, even those who do not know each other, can be partners in the gospel.

We have already noted that a new era of Southern Baptist involvement in Europe began after the London conference of 1920. Dr. Everett Gill, Sr., was appointed by the Foreign Mission Board as its representative to the "new European fields." He believed strongly in cooperation with national Baptist bodies and limitation in Europe of the number of missionaries. The 1923 report of the Foreign Mission Board to the Southern Baptist Convention included the following words from Dr. Gill:

> It is well for us to keep clearly in mind the kind of work we are doing in most of the countries of southern Europe. It is not ordinary missionary work, in the sense of our having originated it and fostered it from the first. In the years gone by and through the labors of others there have grown up and been organized in various lands groups of Baptists. There are, with very few exceptions, no foreign missionaries in these fields, and it is not yet clear that any considerable number should ever be sent. The work of evangelization is being done by the nationals themselves. They can do it infinitely better than foreigners could, and in fact are doing it with gratifying success.
>
> Our work, therefore, is that of strengthening their hands and not that of taking the work out of their hands. Naturally, we, with as much tact as may be given us, counsel with them as to the best methods and principles to be employed in the work. As long as we proceed with good sense and fraternal consideration this co-operation will be a joy to all concerned.

On December 6, 1923, Dr. Gill wrote to Dr. J. F. Love, the corresponding secretary of the Foreign Mission Board, protesting the appointment of a missionary teacher for the Rumanian Baptist Seminary without proper consultation with Rumanian Baptist leaders. He contrasted two methods of doing missionary work: (1) "the usual method of sending missionaries and directing the work from the home office and financing the whole operation" and (2) cooperation between foreign boards and national Baptist organizations, which "plan their own work, do their own evangelizing and are autonomous Baptist bodies." He declared:

> Now, as I have interpreted the minutes of the London conference, and as I have understood from conversations with you all along, I have always had clearly in mind that our Board in this new European work had adopted the cooperative plan. That is, it was not purposed for us to *direct* the work, but that the work was to be carried on by the various national organizations, and we were to cooperate in every possible way.
>
> . . . no one over here has ever contemplated the carrying on of work in Europe as it is done in other lands, that is, by the sending of missionaries and undertaking missionary policies *without the fullest consultation* and agreement with the Boards in Europe.

Dr. Love replied that the Board's policy was one of cooperation, and he said the Board had "not contemplated any large missionary contribution to the European field." However, he added, "I do not think that the Board would be willing to simply turn over money to the European brethren and consider this the extent of the Board's part in this cooperation." It is significant that there was no suggestion that the financial involvement of Southern Baptists in Europe should be related to the number of missionaries there.

There has been tension through the years between the concept that Europe has a special character demanding a special kind of partnership in missions and the concept that missions everywhere consists mainly of sending out and supporting missionaries. The Foreign Mission Board has given, and still gives, high priority to the appointment and support of missionaries, but it has emphasized for a number of years that missionaries have a helping and cooperative function rather than a directive role.

Southern Baptists have the privilege of being partners in the gospel with over one million Baptists in Europe. The Europeans are members of autonomous Baptist churches associated with each other in indigenous Baptist unions. In some countries they have always been independent; elsewhere they have moved from dependence on foreign money and personnel through a stage of reckless independence to a sense of interdependence. The outlook for significant partnership is excellent—if Southern Baptists are ready for it.

Since Southern Baptists did not start Baptist work in most European countries, they have had few temptations to "run the show" in those countries. Even in Italy and Spain, where missionaries once exercised a good bit of authority, the temptations are being resisted (with some prodding by nationals). Churches are now fully self-governing, and the Baptist unions are in charge of denominational matters of common interest. In both countries missionaries have renounced ex officio positions on committees and institutional staffs.

In the October, 1981, meeting of the Foreign Mission Board Dr. Keith Parks said, "We are partners in missions. . . . More and more we will work in a partnership role with strong churches and conventions around the world." This has already happened in Europe.

Missionaries are partners in the gospel with Baptists of twelve European countries. Some missionaries are fully integrated into the national Baptist work, and others have special assignments agreed to by national Baptist leaders.

Several are involved with churches of Americans and/or internationals.

Financial assistance is given to the Baptists of several countries, including some where no Southern Baptist missionaries are stationed (Hungary and Poland, for example). In some countries, Southern Baptists are requested for special short-term assignments. Southern Baptists are welcomed as friends, brothers in Christ, and preachers in such countries as the Soviet Union, where missionaries cannot live and financial assistance cannot be given. The Americans always receive much inspiration and encouragement.

American and European churches are matched up in "partnership evangelism" campaigns in Europe and America. Churches or groups of churches enter into short-term and extended relationships with each other.

The Richmond, Virginia, Baptist Association, for example, in 1982 began a three-year partnership with Portuguese Baptists in evangelistic campaigns. The Oklahoma Baptist Convention entered into a similar partnership with Spanish Baptists. Laymen as well as pastors participate. Per Midteide, the general secretary of the Norwegian Baptist Union, said concerning the effect on church members of a partnership campaign in his country:

> We have seen Christians who never before said anything from the pulpit, or spoke publicly, suddenly have the courage to say something about their relationship to God in the church and to talk to people about Jesus in private homes, schools.

More and more European Baptist leaders are going to America to teach and to preach. The Foreign Mission Board is in partnership with the European Baptist Federation and the various European Baptist unions for the furtherance of the gospel. There is cooperation between Southern Baptists and European Baptists in theological education and other worthwhile endeavors on both international and national levels.

The partnership includes non-Europeans such as American (Northern) Baptists. Even when tensions were high in America between Southern and American Baptists, their representatives in Europe enjoyed a wonderful partnership with each other as well as with European Baptists. The two Baptist bodies of America jointly financed much rebuilding of churches and institutions after World War II.

Planning for Partnership

Partners need to plan together in order to work together effectively. Too often in the past the missionaries in a particular country have made their plans and have hoped the national Baptist body would approve or at least tolerate what was decided; and national Baptists have made their plans, even for missionaries, without consulting the missionaries. Sometimes one group has not even understood the terminology of the other.

Forty-one persons gathered in Ruschlikon, Switzerland, in July of 1981 for a consultation on Baptist work in Europe and the role of Southern Baptists in it. The consultation was called by the Foreign Mission Board area director and his associate in Europe, Dr. Isam Ballenger, who in January of 1982 was to become the director. Seldom has a mission agency convoked such a representative group for counsel about what it should do.

Participants in the consultation included most members of the European Baptist Federation Executive Committee, executive board members of the Baptist Theological Seminary of Ruschlikon, other European Baptist leaders, representatives of the various groups of Southern Baptist missionaries in Europe, two people from the home office staff of the

Foreign Mission Board, one person from the Southern Baptist Convention Executive Committee, and one representative of International Ministries of American Baptist Churches. Of the forty-one participants twenty-two were Europeans from eighteen countries, including five from eastern Europe.

Dr. Knud Wümpelmann, associate secretary of the Baptist World Alliance and general secretary of the European Baptist Federation, began his address on "How Europeans Envision Cooperation with Southern Baptists" by presenting what he called a doodle from a book he picked up once while waiting for a plane. After various suggestions as to what it was, he said, "It is an elephant patting an ant on its shoulder." It was possible then to see the thick leg and foot of an elephant poised above an ant. He said, "It might also suggest the Southern Baptist Convention offering assistance to a little European Baptist union." He added, "We are courageous little ants, and we know Southern Baptists who have shown genuine sensitivity to our situation. This consultation is evidence of that kind of sensitivity." In later discussion he exclaimed, "What is wrong with an elephant that God has created?"

The elephant and the ant are good reminders to Southern Baptists that they can overshadow and even threaten the life of a small Baptist group. However, Dr. Wümpelmann and the other Europeans in the consultation made clear that this is not happening.

The consultation was characterized by a high level of mutual trust. Since missionaries in most countries have never had, and elsewhere do not now have, directive roles, they are not feared. The international ministries supported jointly by European Baptists and Southern Baptists (the Ruschlikon seminary, the Summer Institute of Theological Education, conferences, the European Baptist Press Service, broadcasts, and international evangelistic efforts) pose no threat to any national Baptist group. They meet needs all over Europe, east and west, and help European Baptists to have a sense of unity which is probably unequaled in any other continent.

Since Southern Baptist missionaries are not a threat to nationals, they have wonderful opportunities to use their gifts in support of and alongside nationals. They appreciate the ability, dedication, and trustworthiness of European Baptist leaders, and they are, in turn, trusted and respected.

I stated to the consultation group, "I am committed, and I think my successor will be, to a mission program in Europe which is not independent of organized European Baptist work but is integrated into that work and guided by European Baptist leaders."

Participants in the consultation agreed to present to the Baptist unions of Europe, the European Baptist Federation Council, the Ruschlikon seminary faculty, and the Foreign Mission Board ten concerns for their consideration in planning for the future.

It is significant that the first concern was "that continued assistance be given by the Foreign Mission Board for constructing church buildings and institutions in Europe." The representative of Hungarian Baptists spoke of the importance of church buildings in countries where religious services are permitted only in authorized buildings. Europeans of many countries are indebted to Southern Baptists for help with buildings for churches and institutions. The Foreign Mission Board would do well to plan in such a way that there will always be funds for buildings and current operating expenses, even if this calls for limiting the appointments of missionaries.

Another concern was "that missionary personnel continue to be provided by the Foreign Mission Board when requested by European Baptist unions and that missionaries learn local languages and culture and that national Baptist union representatives be involved in the orientation process." Missionaries are appointed for Europe only when national Baptist leaders in a particular country agree with missionaries in that country that the new missionaries are needed. The need for Europeans (and persons from other parts of the world) to serve in America was recognized. A two-way traffic in missions would express and reinforce genuine partnership.

Two other concerns were "that the Ruschlikon seminary continue to provide theological education for the training of pastors and church leaders and that the area of practical theology be strengthened with special emphasis on evangelism," and "that the Baptist Center of Ruschlikon continue the services of European Baptist Press Service, mass media consultant, conferences, and the SITE program, and that exploration of further development of the Center be pursued with the European Baptist Federation."

Other expressed concerns included assistance in the development and production of literature (especially in Eastern Europe, where there is a great dearth of Baptist literature); a review of selected literature and programs in the area of church growth; and assistance to Baptist unions, upon request, in training national leaders in mass media and videotape production. It was recommended also that ways of service and witness to Muslims in Europe be sought; "that partnership missions be promoted among churches of the European Baptist unions, the European Baptist Convention (English-language), and the Southern Baptist Convention"; and "that opportunities for sharing be provided through exchange programs, including youth, pastors and other church leaders, technical specialists and teachers."

Resolutions urged continued cooperation between Baptist unions and the Foreign Mission Board and proposed "periodic consultations to update our mutual concerns and project new directions for cooperative work."

Baptist partnership in Europe is a wonderful reality. However, it is not a finished product, but rather one that requires cultivation and further development.

3/Baptists in Roman Catholic Countries

The culture of each European country and the character of its people were greatly influenced by the form of Christianity which prevailed in that country. Roman Catholicism, Protestantism, and Eastern Orthodoxy made an imprint which even years of secularism, irreligion, or antireligion have not effaced. To be sure, the differences are less notable today than formerly; but in Scandinavia, for example, there is still a Protestant atmosphere, in Spain a Catholic atmosphere, and in the Soviet Union a suggestion even yet of Orthodoxy.

Europe is the heart of the Roman Catholic world. The papacy is there, and every Pope has been a European. The college of cardinals is overwhelmingly European. Many European countries are traditionally and predominantly Catholic: Italy, Spain, Poland, Portugal, Austria, France, and Belgium. According to statistics released by the Vatican in 1982, Europe had 34.7 percent of the world's Catholics, and 39.9 percent of the population of Europe was Catholic. Many Catholics are found in other European countries. Roman Catholic authorities are trying to make their Church more universal in fact as well as in theory, but for the foreseeable future the center of gravity will likely remain in Europe. It is significant, however, that Europe was the only continent which showed a decline (0.3 percent) between 1970 and 1980 in the percentage of the population belonging to the Catholic Church.

Catholics and Protestants

Western Europe was solidly Roman Catholic until the sixteenth century. Catholic unity was so highly valued that it was protected by persecution, even the expulsion of Jews and other minorities. The Inquisition was used to deal with persons suspected of heresy. Everybody was expected to be an obedient son or daughter of the Church, and most people were.

Religious unity was shattered by the Reformation. When the reformers, who aimed at a reformed church based on the teachings of the Bible, met strong resistance, they decided that the Roman Catholic Church could not be reformed and that new church structures must be built up. They became very anti-Catholic. With the help of ruling princes, the Reformation was established in parts of Germany. Eventually, it was decided that rulers would determine the religion of their realms. The Catholic Church lost parts of central and all of northern Europe. It remained firmly entrenched in Poland, parts of central Europe, and all of southern (Latin) Europe.

After initial hesitation and vacillation, the Roman Catholic Church reacted strongly to the Reformation. Following the Council of Trent (1545-1563), it took an anti-Protestant stance that lasted for more than four centuries, and in some quarters continues. Every possible effort was made to win back individuals and nations. Methods included preaching, writing, the Inquisition, the use of political power, war, and reforming and strengthening the Catholic Church.

The recovery and advance of Catholicism were spearheaded by a new order, the Society of Jesus, created by Ignatius Loyola of Spain to put an army of men at the disposal of the Pope to do his bidding wherever they might be needed. The Jesuits have distinguished themselves by their zeal, learning, diplomacy, and even, according to their enemies, intrigue. At times, including the present, there has been tension between the papacy and the Jesuits.

A general church council, the Council of Trent, was called to deal with the situation created by the Protestant Reformation. It dealt effectively with problems of discipline and morality that had seriously weakened the Church and cost it respect and loyalty. The Roman Catholic Church came out of the experience considerably purified and better organized for its task.

Of particular interest at this point is the fact that the Council of Trent defined Catholic dogma with the specific purpose of condemning Protestant heresy. This sharpened the doctrinal differences between Catholics and Protestants and left few things for discussion or negotiation. Roman Catholic dogma became less flexible. The decisions of the ecumenical Council of Trent as proclaimed by the Pope were not to be abolished. They could only be reinterpreted, and that was not seriously attempted until the 1950s.

What are some of the Catholic dogmas that have proved so offensive to Protestants and that have impelled Baptists to do evangelistic and missionary work among Roman Catholics? The best authoritative statements are found in the canons and decrees of the Council of Trent, issued in 1563.[1]

Contrary to the Protestant principle, tradition as well as the Bible was declared to be authoritative for faith and morals. According to the Council, no one should "interpret the said Scripture contrary to that sense which holy mother Church . . . hath held and doth hold."

The teaching of justification by faith alone was condemned, and the necessity of good works for salvation was affirmed. Without baptism, the sacrament of faith, no one is justified, the Council stated. "If anyone saith, that justifying faith is nothing else but confidence in the divine mercy which remits sins for Christ's sake . . . let him be anathema."

The Council declared that the seven sacraments of baptism, confirmation, Eucharist, penance, extreme unction, ordination, and matrimony confer the grace of God on those who receive them. The baptism of infants was specifically approved as essential for their salvation. Confession of sins to a priest, performing acts indicated by him for the satisfaction of sin, and priestly absolution were parts of the sacrament of penance.

Transubstantiation was declared to take place in the Eucharist: "By the consecration of the bread and of the wine, a conversion is made of the whole substance of the bread into the substance of the body of Christ our Lord, and of the whole substance of the wine into the substance of his blood." The consecrated bread or wine, Christ being present "whole and entire" in both, were declared proper objects of the true worship due the Son of God. Furthermore, affirmed the Council: "If any one saith, that the sacrifice of the mass is only a sacrifice of praise and of thanksgiving; or, that it is a bare commemoration of the sacrifice consummated on the cross, but not a propitiatory sacrifice; or, that it profits him only who receives; and that it ought not be offered for the living and the dead for sins, pains, satisfactions, and other necessities: let him be anathema."

As anathematized persons, under the curse of the Roman Catholic Church, most Protestants reacted in kind. Though they might, like Catholics, accept geographical boundaries for their churches and their religious activities, they usually did not regard Catholics as Christian brothers or the Catholic Church as a true Christian church. The Catholic Church was feared, hated, and combated; its weaknesses were exploited. It was suspected of encouraging all kinds of intrigues and plots in Protestant countries. Only gradually did these feelings subside.

By the nineteenth century, Catholics and Protestants were

reaching a measure of understanding. This was interrupted by the proclamation of two dogmas: the immaculate conception of the virgin Mary (declared to be free from all taint of original sin) and the infallibility of the Pope. Another blow to understanding was the Syllabus of Errors, in which separation of church and state, religious liberty, Bible societies, the idea that "Protestantism is nothing more than another form of the same true Christian religion, in which it is possible to be equally pleasing to God as in the Catholic Church," and other "modern errors" were condemned by Pope Pius IX.[2] At that time, Protestantism seemed to be on the side of progress and understanding, and Catholicism appeared reactionary and intolerant.

Catholics and Baptists

Many of the first Baptists were identified with Protestants. They inherited many Protestant attitudes towards Catholics, but without joining a united Protestant front, since they were often persecuted by Protestants as well as by Catholics. Wherever they met Catholic power, they reacted strongly against the Roman Catholic Church and all it stood for. They sought to rebut Catholic teaching and practices, expose immoralities and irregularities, and show that Rome was an enemy of religious liberty. When they had a chance, as in Ireland under Cromwell, they did their best to win converts from Catholicism. In the course of time, they undertook extensive evangelistic and missionary work among Roman Catholics.

The 1869 report of the Foreign Mission Board to the Southern Baptist Convention expressed concern for Europe and declared: "It is a mournful fact that the wide prevalence of anti-Christian doctrines and forms of worship has rendered many portions of that continent as truly in need of Christian sympathy and missionary enterprise as any portion of the heathen world. Nor is it less true that with our views of the doctrines and ordinances of the gospel, we, as Baptists, are peculiarly qualified to enter and occupy this great field. But especially is it important to note the wonderful openings for missionary labor, which in that field are now presenting themselves."

In 1870 a committee reported to the Southern Baptist Convention as follows: "While we attach great importance to China, India, and Africa, we believe that Italy, Spain, Germany, Mexico, and Ireland are not less inviting as fields for the prosecution of the work of the Board."

For many years there were annual reports to the Southern Baptist Convention on "missions in pagan lands" and "missions in papal lands." The discouragements from opposition and slow progress were recognized, but apparently no one ever questioned the validity of missions in "papal lands."

The following were major reasons for Baptist evangelistic and missionary work in Roman Catholic countries during the nineteenth century and the first half of the twentieth century: (1) Many people in these countries needed the gospel of salvation by the grace of God through faith in Jesus Christ. (2) Many people did not have the Bible or hear biblical preaching. (3) Catholic doctrine impeded true Christian faith and in many respects was contrary to the Bible. (4) Roman Catholicism encouraged superstition. (5) The Catholic Church was an enemy of freedom and progress.

Baptist Development in Roman Catholic Countries

One of the first countries where Baptists appeared was Catholic *Ireland*. Baptist history there goes back to the occupation of the country by Cromwell's English army. Several churches were organized, including one in Dublin that had one hundred and twenty members in 1654. Most of the members were English, however, and when they left Ireland the churches died. For the Irish, it was patriotic to be anti-Protestant, since the English were Protestants; and Ireland became a stronghold of Roman Catholicism.

Most of the 7,900 members of the Baptist Union of Ireland are in Protestant Northern Ireland, with perhaps three hundred in Catholic Eire. They are ultraconservative theologically, and mainly for that reason are not related to the Baptist World Alliance or the European Baptist Federation. They usually register an annual increase in membership.

France was the first country on the continent of Europe to witness the growth of a Baptist community. A man in northern France found an old Bible in his farm home, and he and his neighbors read it. Helped in their understanding by some British soldiers and a man from Switzerland, they were baptized in 1820. This date is not usually given as the beginning of the Baptist movement on the Continent, for the little Baptist church that was formed disappeared after a while.

France was a challenging mission field. It was a traditionally Catholic country with strong anticlerical and even antireligious elements in it. The Catholic Church came close to being overthrown along with the monarchy in the French Revolution. Even before then, the Enlightenment movement had brought widespread skepticism. Adoniram Judson supported the proposal that American Baptists undertake missionary work in France. "An evangelized France," he said, "would stimulate all intelligent classes in Europe." This is not the usual argument for missions, but it is valid. Because France is a cultured nation, it is a strategic mission field. The Reformed Church has a noble history in France, and this has helped to give Protestants respectability.

In 1832 the first American Baptist missionaries sailed for

France. Others followed, but not many. With deaths and resignations, the American missionary "occupation" of France was always on a limited scale and ended after about twenty years. However, the American Baptist Foreign Mission Society continued to give financial assistance and counsel, and for long periods of time its representative to Europe lived in France. British Baptists had missionary work in the Brittany section of France. French Baptists produced some capable, well-educated leaders.

After World War II, Southern Baptists began giving some assistance to French Baptists. In 1960 they sent a missionary to serve as pastor of an English-language church in Orléans. He became the fraternal representative of Southern Baptists to the French Baptist Federation. In 1982, eighteen Southern Baptist missionaries were under assignment to France.

For several years a few Southern Baptist missionaries lived in France to do English-language work and to serve as fraternal representatives to the French Baptist Federation. Southern Baptists' main contribution to French Baptists consisted of funds for buildings and assistance with broadcasting. In the early seventies they began to work more directly with the French people.

At the request of the French Baptist Federation a couple went to Bordeaux in 1976 to plant a church. They rented a building formerly used as a delicatessen and turned it into a Baptist center, which featured a display of books in the window. First, children became curious, and then adults. Bible study groups were formed, and in April, 1977, the first service of worship was conducted. A church was organized several months later.

Similar work has been done by missionaries in Lyons and Toulouse. In the 1981 consultation the representative of French Baptists said, "Creation of churches 'ex nihilo' has been in recent years the work of Southern Baptists. They can do it better than we can."

The French Baptist Federation, which holds membership in the Baptist World Alliance and the European Baptist Federation, in 1981 had about 3,147 members. There are perhaps 1,500 other Baptists in France, most of them theologically "Fundamentalist."

It is not strange that *Italy,* the seat of the papacy, should loom before Baptists as a great missionary challenge. If the gospel as proclaimed by Baptists should gain wide acceptance there, one could hope for remarkable things among Roman Catholics everywhere. The early champions of Baptist missionary work in Italy apparently believed that the whole papal system might collapse, with a mass movement toward evangelical Christianity. They were doomed to disappointment.

In Italy there was far more anticlericalism than interest in a new form of Christianity. Since the papacy blocked the unification of Italy, anticlericalism was patriotic. The movement for independence, which began in the north, reached a climax with the conquest of Rome by Garibaldi in 1870. Protestants had been heartened by his comment that "the Bible is the cannon which shall free Italy." Baptists found the Italian statesman Cavour's advocacy of a free church in a free state appealing. Actually the two men were not particularly interested in religion.

British Baptist missionaries from different groups went to Italy in 1864. Soon the Baptist Missionary Society of England began endeavors that were to continue until they were transferred to Southern Baptists in the early 1920s. An independent Baptist group, the La Spezia Mission, continued much longer.

Italy is one of Southern Baptists' oldest mission fields. Their first representative entered Rome soon after the city was freed from papal rule, and in January, 1871, a church was established there. In 1873 the capable missionary George B. Taylor arrived in Rome, and for thirty-four years he guided Italian Baptist development. Other missionaries went to Italy, but there were never more than two or three couples until after World War II. In 1981, seventeen missionaries were under assignment to Italy. The number was declining.

Nominal Catholics, practicing Catholics, and also some Waldensians, of a pre-Reformation group outside the Catholic Church, have joined Baptist churches. Italian Baptists have contributed to the growth of religious liberty and to the respect enjoyed by Protestants in Italy. A linguistic institute, an orphanage, an old people's home, camps and conferences, broadcasts, and many other projects claim the interest and efforts of Italians and missionaries. However, numerical growth has never been rapid. In 1981, there were about 4,350 members in the Baptist Union of Italy.

Baptist work in Italy has made a painful transition from missionary control to Italian control. The missionary-operated Publishing House has been closed. The valuable property in Rivoli which was bought for a seminary has been turned over to Italian Baptists for a Linguistic School, broadcasting, theological work by correspondence and short-term courses, and other activities. The former Women's Training School property, more recently used as an evangelistic center and hostel under the direction of missionaries Robert and Flora Holifield, will be used for other purposes by Italian Baptists.

Missionaries have given up all directive positions. Italian Baptists will decide whether or not new missionaries will be requested and what they will do. The spirit is good.

There is new enthusiasm for evangelism in Italy, and the Italian people are proving more responsive than they have been in years. A missionary and an Italian are spearheading the evangelistic thrust.

Spain is even more Catholic than Italy. After the expulsion of the Jews and Moors in the late fifteenth and early sixteenth centuries, and the thorough work of the Inquisition when Protestants were discovered in the sixteenth century, the Spanish people were all regarded as Catholics. Even in the 1970s there were only about thirty thousand Protestants and members of Protestant families in Spain. By the 1980s there were perhaps forty-five thousand.

Baptists appeared in Spain after the revolution of 1868 had inaugurated religious liberty for the first time in centuries. A new atmosphere of freedom brought widespread interest in evangelical Christianity. The first Baptist missionary was William Knapp, who after a brief period of independent work became a missionary of the American Baptist Missionary Union (of Northern Baptists). In a period of seven months Knapp enrolled 1,325 professed converts. However, when he organized a church in Madrid in August, 1870, only thirty-three persons were ready for membership. Several other churches were established, but after the missionary withdrew in 1876 they disappeared.

The Baptist witness in Spain was resumed in the area of Barcelona under Swedish and American Baptist sponsorship, and a bit later in the region of Valencia with Swedish Baptist missionary assistance. Restrictions on religious liberty prevailed most of the time, and Catholic resistance to Protestant teaching prevailed all of the time. Still, churches were established, and by 1920 there were six hundred Baptists in the country. Following the London conference of Baptist leaders in 1920, Southern Baptists sought to unify and promote the work formerly sponsored by other Baptist groups.

Serious financial problems made it impossible for Southern Baptists to do all they had planned in any of their mission fields. Expansion in Spain, as elsewhere, was followed by retrenchment. Establishment of the Spanish republic in 1931 brought freedom but also anticlericalism and religious indifference. The victory of General Franco in the civil war in 1939 brought the closing of almost all Baptist churches.

A new era of expansion began in 1945, when religious toleration was granted Protestants; churches could be opened again. The period proved to be one of limited toleration. During the decade beginning in 1948 several churches were closed, and Protestant activities were limited.

The denials of freedom were not great enough to destroy Protestantism, but they were well enough known to gain sympathy for Protestants. Baptists reopened their seminary, acquired some valuable church property, engaged in clandestine publication work, preached in their churches, and did extensive personal evangelistic work. Their period of limited toleration was a time of unprecedented growth. They increased from 1,510 members in 1948 to 2,720 ten years later. By October, 1981, they numbered 5,966.

Broad religious toleration became the law of the land when a new constitution was adopted in 1966. A law on "religious liberty" the following year called upon Protestant "associations" (churches) to register, and guaranteed registered churches more extensive rights than they had enjoyed for many years. However, many churches refused to register because of the requirement that they submit their membership rolls and financial records to government inspection. Serious tension developed among Baptists because of differences of opinion concerning strategy, but this subsided.

A new era for Spain began in 1975 with the death of Franco and the ascendancy of Juan Carlos. With determination and political acumen, the new king made Spain a constitutional monarchy which practices democracy (though threatened by extremists).

A new constitution was approved by the Cortes, ratified by the Spanish people, and promulgated by the king in 1978. It established religious liberty to a degree never known before in Spanish history. A new law specifying the meaning in practice of religious liberty was passed in 1980. All religions now enjoy full freedom in Spain.

One point that was cleared up by the new law was the ownership of property by churches and religious associations. In 1981, the Foreign Mission Board put Baptist lands and buildings (except for missionary residences and properties of several churches that wanted the Foreign Mission Board to continue as the legal owner) in the names of churches or the Spanish Baptist Union. This was a pledge of confidence by Southern Baptists in Spanish Baptists and the acceptance by Spanish Baptists of the responsibilities of maturity.

The achievement of religious liberty has been accompanied by growing secularism and religious indifference in Spain, and Protestant growth has been somewhat limited. Baptists began in 1978 a five year plan for the strengthening of weak churches and the establishment of new ones. Things have been done (radio programs, meetings in public places, and massive literature distribution) which would have been impossible under Franco. A new missionary program of expansion continues the five year emphasis and adds new features within Spain plus the development of a foreign mission program in Equatorial Guinea in cooperation with Southern Baptists and perhaps other Baptist groups.

One of the most encouraging features of Baptist work in Spain has been the development of new churches in pioneer situations by missionaries and Spaniards. Spanish Baptist leaders are urging the appointment of new missionaries for this kind of work.

Southern Baptist financial assistance in Spain has been considerable. Usually missionaries have been well received and have played an important role in Spanish Baptist development. Until the 1950s Southern Baptists usually had only one or two missionary couples in Spain. By 1982, there were forty-seven missionaries under assignment there. They were helpers of Spanish Baptists rather than directors of the work.

Portugal was even less affected by the Reformation than was Spain. The overwhelming majority of its citizens are Catholics. When Salazar became dictator in 1933, he set out to make Portugal a Catholic state founded on the religious, political, and social principles of papal encyclicals. There was a close alliance, without actual union, of church and state. Protestants were not suppressed, but they were watched, limited, and controlled by the authorities. The dictatorship has given way to democracy and religious freedom.

Portugal's Baptists owe their origin to British and Brazilian influence. In 1888 some baptisms by immersion took place. In 1908 a new Baptist start was made with the help of a Southern Baptist missionary to Brazil. He was sent to Portugal by the newly organized Brazilian Baptist Convention. In subsequent years several Brazilian missionaries had regular assignments to Portugal.

Growth was slow, and divisions took place. One of the most serious divisions occurred in 1945 when the Conservative Baptist Foreign Mission Society began giving assistance in Portugal. In time this schism was more or less healed, but another took place about 1955 when a Landmark Baptist group from America led some churches in establishing a Portuguese Baptist Association.

Brazilian Baptists continued their interest in Portugal but were unable to give much help. In 1959 the Southern Baptist Foreign Mission Board heeded a request for assistance made by the Portuguese Baptist Convention with the endorsement of the Brazilian Baptist Convention. Fraternal representatives took up residence in Portugal and financial assistance was given, especially for buildings. New Brazilian missionaries went to Portugal in the 1970's. A good three-way partnership developed among them, Southern Baptist representatives, and Portuguese Baptists. In 1982 there were eighteen Southern Baptist missionaries in Portugal.

During the 1960s and 1970s much progress was made toward unity among Portuguese Baptists. Good growth took place. Churches of the convention had three thousand members by 1981—triple the number they had twenty years earlier. There are still several Baptist churches outside the convention.

In 1967, for the first time in the history of Portuguese Baptists, a radio program was begun over transmitters reaching all of the country. It has been well received. In 1968 a Baptist book store was opened on a busy street in Lisbon. During the following year a seminary with a student body of eight held its first session, and several years later property was bought with the help of Southern Baptists.

One of the most successful nationwide campaigns ever conducted in Portugal took place in May, 1981. The pastors and members of the Portuguese Baptist churches did the planning and most of the work. Over twenty Baptist pastors from Brazil went at the expense of their local churches to preach in Portugal. Besides services in local churches, there were mass meetings in Lisbon and Porto. Southern Baptists supplied money for renting meeting places, preparing literature, and advertising the meetings. Over twelve hundred first-time decisions for Christ were made.

The Hapsburg rulers of *Austria* held the title of Holy Roman Emperor for nearly four hundred years, ending in 1804. They ruled a great empire in central Europe. In most of the Austrian domain the Reformation made much progress, but a counterreformation brought most of the population back into the Catholic Church.

After World War I, several nations were carved out of the

Austro-Hungarian Empire, and Austria was left as a small country. About 90 percent of its population of 7,000,000 is Catholic.

In 1969 the Baptist church on the Mollardgasse (Mollard Street) in Vienna celebrated its centennial. The first leader and preacher of the church was a representative of the British and Foreign Bible Society. German Baptists and, later, German American Baptists gave assistance. For about eighty years the church in Vienna was the only one in the present territory of Austria. For a long time it was not recognized by the authorities and had frequent difficulties.

After World War II several new churches were established. In the 1960s an international committee with a German Baptist chairman was organized to promote Baptist work in Austria. In agreement with Austrian Baptist leaders and this committee, Southern Baptists sent a couple as fraternal representatives to Austria in 1965. The missionaries opened a youth center in Salzburg and worked with the churches and with young people throughout the country. In 1982 there were twelve Southern Baptist missionaries under assignment to Austria. Though Austrian Baptists numbered only 695 in 1981, they were planning hopefully for the future.

Another Catholic country that should be mentioned is *Belgium*. French influence is responsible for the origin of Baptists there. In spite of religious freedom, little progress has been made. In 1971 there were about seven hundred thirty Baptists in the country. Evangelism there is a special project of the European Baptist Federation. The Southern Baptist Foreign Mission Board and the American Baptist Foreign Mission Society give financial help. The latter Society has a missionary couple at work in the country, and seven Southern Baptist missionaries are assigned to work with English-language congregations and assist Belgium Baptists in evangelism, church development, and youth work.

In the seven countries dealt with, excluding northern Ireland, there are fewer than seventeen thousand Baptists. Nowhere has a breakthrough such as that in Brazil occurred. Will it take place? No one can be sure. It is clear that the weakness of Baptists in Catholic countries underlines the need of partnership with others in sharing the gospel.

A New Era

A new era for Roman Catholicism and for Catholic-Protestant relations began with Pope John XXIII. Instead of pronouncing anathemas on Protestants, he referred to them as separated and beloved Christian brothers. Determined to let fresh air into the Catholic Church, he called Vatican Council II and permitted the assembled bishops to say things that would have been unthinkable a few years earlier. Protestants accepted invitations to send observers to the Council, and even some Baptists were present.

The Council was convoked not to change Catholic dogma but rather, as Pope John said, to guard it and determine how to teach it more efficaciously. The fact that the second sentence of Pope John's opening address to the Council in 1962 referred to "the Virgin Mother of God" and that almost the last words to the Council from Pope Paul VI in 1965 exalted "Mary Most Holy, the Immaculate One" made quite clear that the official position of the virgin Mary among Catholics remained unchanged. Some dogmas were reaffirmed; others were simply taken for granted. The reaffirmations of dogma, since they were not made in opposition to Protestant teaching, appear more conciliatory than the decisions at Trent. The debates in the Council made abundantly clear that many matters of doctrine have not been solidified into dogma and that even dogma can be reinterpreted.

The sacraments remain the same, but (even though it was said that they impart grace) personal faith and personal response to God's grace take on greater importance. Permission was given for the Eucharist to be celebrated in common languages of the people rather than in Latin only. Other significant changes in rites and ceremonies were made. Keen sensitivity to conditions in the world and Christian responsibility for the world were demonstrated. The Catholic Church went far toward erasing the impression of being an obstacle to progress. Liberal, progressive forces in the Church proved to be stronger than most people had suspected.

Without abandoning tradition as an authoritative guide for the Church, the Council exalted the Scriptures. This was in line with growing biblical scholarship among Catholics and with new efforts to give people the Bible in their own language. Since the Council, Catholics and Protestants have been able in several places to unite in Bible translation and distribution. Of course, many Catholics are still ignorant of the Bible, as are many Baptists, but it is not by the will of their Church.

For centuries, repression of non-Catholics in Catholic lands was supported by statements from Popes and other persons of authority; but, fortunately, there was never a decision by an ecumenical council or an "ex cathedra" statement from a Pope denying the validity of religious liberty. Papal encyclicals are not generally considered "ex cathedra," or infallibly binding always on all people. Vatican Council II supported religious liberty. The old right of truth to be protected by state powers from error was replaced by the right of persons to act according to conscience. After this declaration it would be difficult for enemies of religious liberty even in Spain to maintain that their position and attitudes were the proper ones for Roman Catholics. New legislation in Spain on religious liberty is a direct result of the new teaching of the Catholic church. Although prejudices, injustices, and inequalities will continue, severe persecution of Christians by other Christians is hopefully a thing of the past.

Roman Catholics now participate in joint discussion groups and, indeed, in acts of worship with Baptists and other Protestants. A Baptist seminary professor from America has been guest professor in the Gregorian University of Rome. A Southern Baptist missionary has taken part on a panel in the University of Salamanca, Spain. The Baptist secretary of the Protestant Defense Committee of Spain has addressed meetings of leaders of church and state, and when a new Constitutional Court was inaugurated by King Juan Carlos in 1980, he attended as a guest of honor along with a representative of the Jews and a Catholic cardinal. A Spanish Baptist has lectured on Baptists in the Autonomous University of Madrid, and his lectures were attended by the queen.

What about the position of the Pope? Vatican Council II left untouched the Pope's supreme authority and his infallibility when solemnly proclaiming dogma. However, it also exalted the function and the authority of bishops—to be exercised with the consent of the Pope. The bishops and the Pope together, or the Pope alone, may declare a teaching to be a part of revelation and therefore binding on the faithful.

Since Vatican Council II, pressure has built up for the Pope to share more of his authority with the bishops. At the same time priests and laymen are asking for a greater voice in decisions within the church. This may be a natural development of the Council's definition of the church as the people of God. The Roman Catholic Church is far less centralized and authoritarian than it was.

Strong winds of change are blowing. One suspects that

the successors of John XXIII would like to close some of the windows that he opened, or that have been blown open since. There is reformation, revolution, and revival in the Roman Catholic Church.

Catholic dogma is being challenged from within the Church itself. Interesting new ideas are expressed. Some, such as "transignification" (proposed by some Dutch theologians as a substitute for transubstantiation), have been condemned. Others enjoy free discussion.

In the realm of discipline there is serious and widespread resistance to authority. Opposing the Vatican in the area of doctrine is only one step beyond disobedience in matters of discipline. Pope Paul VI offended many members of the hierarchy by his condemnation of birth control in spite of the recommendation of a study commission he had appointed. The reaction of many laymen has been that such things are outside the jurisdiction of the Pope, bishops, and priests.

The bishops of Holland have openly opposed the Pope on clerical celibacy. Cardinal Suenens of Belgium called for open dialogue among the bishops on this question. The Pope expressed "grieved astonishment" at comments made by bishops who, he said, seemed to lack a brotherly spirit. A new Dutch catechism was disapproved by the Vatican. Even papal infallibility is being questioned by some and reinterpreted by many.

What is the future of the Roman Catholic Church in Europe? While it will have less temporal power and wealth and will experience a decline in membership, its stature and its inner vitality will probably grow. There is a good likelihood that it will emerge from its travail stronger and more missionary than ever before.

What about Baptist mission work in Roman Catholic

countries, and among Roman Catholics elsewhere? Is it still justified?

Certainly one could not insist that the Catholic Church withholds the Bible from its members or deny that much biblical, even evangelical, preaching takes place in Catholic churches. Instead of denouncing the biblical ignorance of Catholics, all might join with them in a search for biblical truth, perhaps using Bibles approved by the Catholic Church. Such an approach to the Bible would open the way for dialogue, with participants respecting one another and being ready for the acceptance of truth.

Even while admiring much Catholic teaching and rejoicing in the correction of Catholic doctrine in the light of the Bible, Protestants see dogmas and practices that challenge them to share with Catholics the Christian message as they understand it. Evangelical teaching needs to be put over against papal infallibility, the cult of the virgin Mary, prayers to saints, and transubstantiation. Basic elements of the Christian message need emphasis: salvation by the grace of God through faith in Christ; the right of the individual to go directly into the presence of God without the mediation of priests, saints, or sacraments; the personal nature of true religion; the right of the individual to interpret the truth of God.

Many people in Catholic countries need the Christian gospel. Some of them have never been practicing Catholics. Many are thoroughly secularized. Some are quite anti-Catholic or even anti-religious. More than once in Catholic countries of Europe seething opposition to the Catholic Church has burst out in the burning of churches and the killing of priests. Furthermore, many peaceful, law-abiding citizens—some atheists and others believers in God—never think of attending Mass or seeking any of the services of the church. These people usually cannot be reached by the

Catholic Church, but some of them are open to the Christian gospel proclaimed and lived by those who aren't Catholics.

Some who need to hear the gospel are faithful Catholics. Even a faithful Baptist may not be a Christian, and the number of Catholics who have not had any kind of personal Christian experience is high, especially in countries where almost everyone considers himself a Catholic. The way of salvation is not presented with sufficient clarity, and the way to God may be cluttered with superstitions, ceremonies, and saints.

After Vatican Council II, opposition to Protestants in Catholic countries will not be violent, and Protestants must learn to live without the stimulation of harassment. They will not be regarded as demons and will therefore have a chance to show whether they have a message and a way of life that are worth sharing. Some of the rebels in the Catholic Church may turn to Protestant churches. Will they find the freedom they so earnestly seek and also truth which they can accept and live by?

Let there be no doubt of the continuing need of missions to Catholic countries. We must not be belligerent in our approach, but neither should we be apologetic. We have a message that is needed by the whole world, and our obligation is to give it to those who need it, wherever they may be. Those who accept it will have new opportunities for active and constructive participation in the life of their communities and nations.

Notes

1. See Philip Schaff, ed., *The Creeds of Christendom,* Vol. 2 (New York: Harper, 1919).

2. Ibid., p. 217 f.

4/Baptists in Protestant Lands

In Worms, Germany, stands an impressive monument to Martin Luther, who shook Christendom to its foundations and inadvertently created a new expression of Christianity. Around the statue of Luther are gathered statues of theologians, princes, and other persons who helped him usher in a new era. At Worms in 1521, standing before the emperor and the spiritual and temporal lords of the Holy Roman Empire, Luther said that his conscience was captive to the Word of God and that he could not recant anything he had taught unless convicted by Scripture and plain reason. "Here I stand. I cannot do otherwise."

In Geneva, Switzerland, a monument of the Reformation impressively depicts John Calvin and some of his spiritual kinsmen of various lands. Easily recognizable are John Knox, who made Scotland Presbyterian; the Puritan Oliver Cromwell of England; and the Baptist Roger Williams of America. Not forgotten are Luther and Zwingli, who are commemorated by detached blocks inscribed with their names.

Near the Grossmünster church in Zurich, Switzerland, stands a statue of Ulrich Zwingli, who from this church led his part of the nation into the Reformation. In one hand he holds a Bible, for he was a preacher and theologian; in the other, he holds a sword, for he was a soldier who died fighting with his people against fellow Swiss who stayed in the Roman Catholic Church.

Not far from the statue is the place in the Limmat River

where Anabaptist Felix Manz was executed by drowning, with Zwingli's consent, because Manz taught that only believers should be baptized and become church members. The Anabaptists represented an expression of Protestantism that seemed to most of their contemporaries, both Protestants and Catholics, radical and even dangerous. Baptists, though not directly descended from Anabaptists, are glad to claim spiritual kinship with them.

The Reformation

No wonder monuments were erected to leaders of the Reformation. It was an earth-shaking movement. It shattered the religious unity of western Europe; it changed the course of history; and it made a tremendous impact on civilization. How different the world would be today if the Reformation had not taken place!

The Reformation was the greatest religious upheaval that had occurred in many centuries—and it was a part of a radical change in society. There had been earlier protests against Roman Catholic doctrine, but Luther and the other reformers broke through the whole Roman Catholic system by their discovery that, according to the New Testament, salvation is only by the grace of God through faith in Jesus Christ. That being true, they insisted that the "good works" represented by pilgrimages, fasting, penance, masses for the dead, and indulgences are not of decisive importance. Furthermore, if the grace of God is experienced by those who have faith (which means trust, confidence, and commitment to God), man is not dependent on grace-imparting sacraments or on people who administer them. Since this is so, some reformers determined, all are priests and all are the laity (meaning people of God), though there are different forms of service. This kind of reasoning opened the whole clerical system—from priests to bishops to Pope—for free examination to determine whether or not it was serving God and the church.

The reformers appealed to the Scriptures in their challenge to traditional Roman Catholic faith and practice. Some were ready to go further than others in following the Bible, but all thought the church should be emancipated from the tyranny of tradition. They preached and taught the Bible, and they translated it for the people. Studying the Bible had made them reformers, and they were convinced that it would lead other people to become Protestants.

However, this can be a slow process. Most of the well-known reformers were quite willing to accept the help of temporal powers in achieving religious reform. Zwingli decided to move at the pace set by the Zurich city council. Luther leaned heavily on "Christian princes," including at least one very immoral man, to establish the Reformation in Germany. King Henry VIII severed the ties of the English Church with Rome when the Pope refused to grant him a divorce. The English kings and the Lutheran kings of several countries became the supreme rulers of established churches in their lands. Calvin and Calvinists were less inclined to subordinate the church to the state, but in Presbyterian and Reformed countries there was also a close alliance of church and state. Only the radical reformers, the Anabaptists, opposed this and insisted that churches should be autonomous congregations of believers baptized on profession of their faith in Christ.

Bloody civil conflicts and wars between nations followed the Reformation. They can be traced in part to political rivalries, ambitions of rulers, and growing national loyalties; but Catholics lined up on one side and Protestants on the other. The result of the wars was that Catholicism was left dominant in some countries and Protestantism in others, while still other countries were divided along religious lines. In most places people were expected to follow the established religion. National churches were supported by state funds. In some countries religious minorities were tolerated.

Differences of custom, conduct, and culture appeared and continued even after the decline of religion. Many popular religious festivals were abolished where Protestantism became dominant; life became more serious and, some would say, more somber. Work, frugality, honesty, and education were emphasized. The Protestant environment was favorable for the development of science, free enterprise, material progress, and also materialism and secularism. Modern world culture owes many of its features, good and bad, to Protestantism.

Protestants and Baptists in Europe Today

Most European Protestants are members of what the Germans call Volkskirchen, churches of the people or mass churches. They are so identified with the nation that most citizens belong more or less automatically to them. If someone in Zurich is asked, "Are you a Christian?" he will probably respond, "Of course; I am Swiss." That is true even if he never goes to church. Infant baptism admits most people to mass churches, but Swedish parentage is sufficient in Sweden, even without baptism.

The leading churches once enjoyed exclusive rights and privileges as established churches. Union of church and state was as characteristic of Protestant countries as of Catholic, and some Protestant churches were even more subservient to the state than the Roman Catholic Church was. Religious minorities were oppressed. However, the conviction that this was contrary to the spirit of Protestantism gradually gained strength, and since the latter part of the nineteenth century there has been no Protestant religious oppression.

Lutheranism is the established religion in the Scandinavian countries. Its status is a grade lower in Protestant sections of Germany, but there also it receives financial support from state-levied taxes. The Anglican Church is the "Church of England," with certain clerical appointments and even the forms of worship subject to state control. The Presbyterian Church is the "Church of Scotland," but it is more autonomous than the Church of England. The Reformed Church (Presbyterian) in the Netherlands has the prestige of a once-dominant church, and the Reformed Church in certain cantons of Switzerland receives government financial support and enjoys a special place in Swiss society.

Serious discussions on church-state separation are taking place. Many irreligious people want it; however, some who are not actively religious think the church should be maintained by the state because of its historical and cultural significance and because of its services on such occasions as marriage and death. Some churchmen advocate separation of church and state so the church will become more independent, will call for more loyalty and support from its members, and will, in fact, become more a church. When in 1969 a nonofficial but representative assembly of the Norwegian Lutheran Church voted 145 to 25 against state-church separation, one of the twenty-five (Norway's youngest bishop) called the present arrangement a narcotic and a means of escape from reality.

In several countries steps have been taken toward equalizing financial support for churches. Baptist institutions and even churches have become eligible for help from governments, and they have sometimes accepted it. A religious liberty law enacted in Norway in 1969 provides for turning over to recognized "free churches" (to denominational headquarters and congregations) the church tax included in income tax payments by members of those churches. One senses in parts of Europe a trend toward what might be called a multiple establishment of religions, with state aid to all that are officially recognized. Some people think this poses a threat to the autonomy of Baptist churches, and also to their self-sufficiency, since the generosity of members may decrease if the church has other sources of income. It may violate the religious freedom of irreligious persons, whose numbers are increasing rapidly, or of members of small, unrecognized groups who cannot reach into the public treasury.

The traditional Protestant churches have made great contributions to Europe. There is still much strength in them and potential for the good of Europe. An indication of strength in the rather small Swiss Reformed Church is the fact that it produced Karl Barth and Emil Brunner, the two most influential theologians during several decades of the twentieth century. How could anyone say that the Swiss Reformed Church is dead?

Professor Brunner was once asked whether he saw in Europe signs of a popular revival of religion that would correspond to the revival of European theology. His reply was negative.

Revival is needed. It has come before when the need was most urgent. Will it come again? If it comes, will it take place within existing church structures or outside them? Will it be socially as well as personally oriented?

Baptists got started in Europe when people were searching for a satisfying personal religious faith and vital Christian experience. The formal Anglicanism of the seventeenth century and the arid orthodoxy and vacillating liberalism of the nineteenth century on the Continent were inadequate for many people, and some of these people became Baptists.

Baptists have made a place for themselves in all of the Protestant countries of Europe. They started there before their development in Catholic countries, and their growth has been far greater among Protestants than among Catholics.

Unfortunately, Baptists, as well as other religious groups, have suffered attrition from the secularism of our age. Prayer services and revival meetings that appealed to Pietists of the nineteenth century usually do not interest modern secular man.

British Baptists

Baptist history goes back further in England than anywhere else. Baptists arose from among English Separatists in the early seventeenth century. Out of the religious turmoil of that period appeared Puritans who wanted to reform the Anglican Church along Calvinistic lines. From among the Puritans came those who were more radical still and separated from the state church as Separatists or Independents. In time, they fused with other Puritans as Congregationalists. Among the Separatists, who were always looking for "more truth yet to break forth out of God's holy Word," there were people who decided that the Bible taught the baptism of believers. They organized churches on this principle.

The move to the Baptist position was begun by some English refugees in Holland. They were led by John Smyth, who was educated as an Anglican minister, and by Thomas Helwys, a country gentleman trained in law. In 1609 Smyth baptized himself by pouring water on his head, and then he baptized Helwys and about forty other persons who were ready to join in the creation of a new church. Shortly thereafter, Smyth became troubled concerning his self-baptism and decided that he should have turned to the Mennonites who practiced believer's baptism. He died before negotiations with the Mennonites were completed, but some of his followers joined them. In 1611 or 1612,

Helwys and a group of eight or ten persons who wanted to keep themselves distinct from the Mennonites returned to England and established a Baptist church in Spitalfield, just outside London's walls.

Thus began the General Baptists, so called because of their Arminian belief in a general atonement, the effects of which reach all who have faith in Christ. A few years later the Particular Baptist movement started. It was so called because of a strict Calvinistic belief that the atonement was limited in its effects to particular persons divinely pre-destined to be saved. The first church of this type was formed about 1638. Eventually the differences between the two types of Baptists became less sharp, and they com-bined. Baptism by immersion began to be practiced by Baptists about 1641. The importance of baptizing the right persons, believers, was grasped before the form was re-garded as important.

One of the most influential men produced by British Baptists was William Carey, who inaugurated a new era in foreign missions. Convinced that Christians are obligated to share their knowledge of the gospel to the ends of the earth, he challenged his fellow believers to "expect great things from God" and "attempt great things for God." A Baptist missionary society was formed in 1792, and Carey and John Thomas were sent to India. This aroused the interest and pricked the consciences of Christians everywhere, and other missionaries were sent out.

Another great figure in British Baptist history is Charles Haddon Spurgeon, who was a pastor in London during the second half of the nineteenth century. Great crowds of people gathered regularly to hear him preach—as many as twenty-three thousand persons on one occasion. His ser-mons were printed each week, and more than one hundred million of them have been sold. His great mission in life was to win the lost through preaching and personal witnessing. He is honored by British Baptists as their prince of preachers.

The peak of British Baptist membership and influence was reached early in the twentieth century. In 1906 membership in England, Scotland, and Wales was reported to be 434,741. Except for momentary spurts forward, a decline set in after that, and it gained momentum after World War II. In only a few recent years has growth been registered. In 1981 the Baptist World Alliance reported 170,999 Baptists affiliated with the Baptist Union of Great Britain and Ireland, which in actual fact does not now include Ireland or Scotland. There were perhaps 100,000 additional Baptists in the United Kingdom.

Most denominations are having a hard time in Great Britain. Large church buildings stand in places where there are few people, and no churches are to be found in some new urban areas and housing developments. More serious is the prevailing irreligious climate. It is no longer easy to attract a crowd to hear the gospel, nor is it easy to present the gospel understandably, acceptably, and appealingly.

Many British Baptists are seeking earnestly to show the relevance of Christianity to life today. They are well informed and open-minded. There is also great concern for spiritual renewal and evangelism. After a 1970 simultaneous evangelistic campaign in Scotland, Scottish Baptists' general secretary said: "Some churches had lost confidence in their ability to win people to Christ. Now they have renewed confidence that they can."

English Baptists are not candidates for missionary assistance but, instead, send missionaries elsewhere. However, Southern Baptists have had the opportunity to assist with several special projects. One was helping Spurgeon's College establish a lectureship in evangelism by providing funds for the lecturer's salary on a decreasing scale over a period of five years. Another was financial assistance with an evangelism center in Manchester.

In recent years very fruitful cooperation has developed between Southern Baptists and the Baptists of *Scotland*. This was largely an achievement of Reverend Andrew Mac-Rae, the former secretary of the Scottish Baptist Union, who was well known in America as a preacher in churches and guest lecturer in theological seminaries. Southern Baptists have aided in WIN Schools and evangelistic campaigns, in religious education, in office work, in youth work and music, and in pastorates. An International Baptist Church, made up mainly of American and Scottish workers in the oil industry, and a new church made up mainly of Scots have been organized by Southern Baptist missionaries.

Scottish Baptists have been welcomed in Southern Baptist Churches and denominational headquarters, and further visits are planned. They, in turn, have welcomed Mission Service Corps workers, short-term specialists, journeymen, and career missionaries.

Reverend Gilbert Ritchie, who represented Scottish Baptists in the 1981 consultation, said that they today have such an opportunity as they have never had. Following a gradual decline in strength for about fifty years, there are now signs of life: many young people in the churches, an excellent supply of young men for the ministry, a remarkable growth in giving, an encouraging improvement in church attendance, new churches, and an increase in baptisms. He said, "We owe much to Southern Baptists for their encouragement, inspiration, and practical help."

In 1981 there were 14,633 members of churches affiliated with the Baptist Union of Scotland (and 1,832 in unaffiliated churches). There were two career missionaries and three journeymen assigned to Scotland.

German and Dutch Baptists

In spite of the facts that there were Anabaptists in Reformation times and that English Baptists arose in Holland in the seventeenth century, Baptists did not take root on the European continent until the nineteenth century. Their origin is due largely to British and American influence and to independent study of the Bible.

In 1834 Johann Gerhard Oncken was baptized in Hamburg, *Germany,* and a Baptist church was organized. He received financial help from American Baptists for missionary work in Germany and other countries but worked quite independently. By the time of his death, fifty years after his baptism, there were more than thirty thousand Baptists in the "Germany Mission," including at least eight countries besides Germany.

The remarkable growth was probably due to the following factors: (1) There was spiritual hunger in Germany because churches were suffering from rationalism and indifference. (2) Pietism prepared the way for the Baptist emphasis on personal religious experience, and in some cases formed groups that readily became Baptist. (3) The Baptist movement was indigenous. (4) There were capable Baptist leaders (including Oncken, Julius Köbner, who was the son of a Danish rabbi, and Gottfried Wilhelm Lehmann of Berlin). (5) There was a spirit of missions, inspired by Oncken's conviction that every Baptist should be a missionary.

Baptists faced strong opposition during the first few years of their existence. A government official in Hamburg once said to Oncken: "As long as I can lift this little finger, you will feel the force of it." Oncken replied: "I believe you do not see what I see. You see only your own arm. But I am not looking at that. I see a great arm, and that is the arm of God.

So long as that arm moves, you will never silence me."
From the middle of the nineteenth century, Baptists had few complaints against German authorities.

One of the worst times for Baptists was during Nazi rule. Their personal liberties and the freedom of churches were circumscribed. However, Baptist leaders avoided a direct confrontation with the regime.

German Baptists have long cooperated in a union, which since 1940-41 includes some Plymouth Brethren and mild Pentecostals. It is known as the Federation of Evangelical Free-Church Congregations. Even after the division of Germany following World War II the one union continued; but in 1969, accepting the fact that joint effort was impossible, the Baptists of East Germany organized their own Federation of Evangelical Free Churches of the German Democratic Republic. At that time there were 25,000 Baptists in East Germany and 67,500 in West Germany.

German Baptists faced a tremendous problem of reconstruction after World War II. Among those who went to their aid were American (Northern) Baptists and Southern Baptists. Many church buildings, the seminary in Hamburg, and the publishing house in Kassel were rebuilt.

The seminary in Hamburg is one of the largest Baptist seminaries on the continent of Europe, with an average enrollment of about sixty-five. Oncken began giving short courses for mission workers in 1849. The actual founding of the seminary, however, took place in 1880, when six students were enrolled for a four-year course. The division of the country led to the establishment in 1959 of a smaller seminary in Bukow for students in East Germany.

Deaconesses constitute an unusual feature of German and Swiss Baptist life. Most of them are nurses, but some have assignments with young people. Several large deaconess houses afford training and opportunities of service for Baptist women.

For many years German Baptists were limited mainly to the Protestant sections of their country. This changed after World War II, when Baptist refugees from what had been East Prussia and from what became the German Democratic Republic settled in Catholic areas of West Germany. The Baptist appeal to people who have grown up as Roman Catholics is still limited, but a beginning has been made.

Baptists in West Germany, with 68,489 members in 1981, are holding their own numerically. In East Germany, formerly one of the most Protestant of all lands, Baptists grew under Communist rule until 1952, but since then they have lost several thousand members. An East German Baptist leader, referring to the rapid secularization of life in his country, said: "The Christian church is thrown back to fundamental questions: What is she? What does she have? What does she want? Where is she going?"

German Baptists want Southern Baptists to move ahead with them. Whereas most Southern Baptist missionaries have heretofore worked with English-language churches, German Baptist leaders in 1981 requested two American missionary couples to do pioneer work with Germans and a couple to join Germans and Americans in an outreach to Muslims in Germany, especially with Turks, of whom there are probably 1,250,000 in the country. The first two couples were appointed in 1982.

The Baptist movement in *Holland* owed much in its early years to Germany. After Johannes Feisser had been dismissed as a Reformed pastor because of his criticism of the church and his refusal to baptize infants or administer communion to unbelievers, Oncken and Köbner made contact with him. In 1845 he and six other persons were baptized and formed a Baptist church. Several other churches were established through German Baptist influence. However, independence, and also English influence, was strong among early Dutch Baptists.

In 1881 the Union of Baptist Churches in the Netherlands was founded. A bit later it joined the German Baptist Union for a while, but without vote or the right of Dutchmen to hold office. Most Dutch Baptist preachers were trained in Hamburg, but some were trained also in England.

Since 1958 Dutch Baptists have had their own seminary. It established a good cooperative relationship with a nearby university, as have Baptist seminaries in Great Britain. The rector of the seminary is also on the theological faculty of the university.

Dutch Baptists register steady annual gains in membership. By the beginning of 1981, there were 12,055 members in eighty-one churches.

English-Language Churches

Since the mid-1950s, English-language Baptist churches have been formed in many places overseas where Americans live. Other denominations, especially Episcopalians and Presbyterians, began much sooner than Baptists to provide a spiritual ministry to Americans living away from home. Once the movement started among Baptists it rapidly gained momentum.

In 1981 there were forty-three English-language Baptist churches and mission points in Europe. The average membership was eighty. Most of the churches were self-supporting. Only seven had their own buildings. Others rented property or shared national Baptist buildings. Half of the churches belonged to a national Baptist union as well as to the European Baptist Convention. The majority of the churches were in Germany; two were in Austria; two in Belgium; four in England; one in Scotland; one in France; one in Greece; two in the Netherlands; three in Italy; one in Norway; three in Spain; and one in Portugal.

In the majority of the churches, most of the members are

American military personnel and their families. However, this is not the case in Paris, Brussels, Innsbruck, Salzburg, Rome, Stavanger, or Aberdeen. Everywhere, good relationships with local people have been established. Several churches are truly international. In 1981, the church in Brussels was said to include twenty-seven nationalities.

The churches are related to one another through the European Baptist Convention (English-language), which has Southern Baptist missionaries as general secretary, youth director, and religious education specialist. The convention is affiliated with the European Baptist Federation.

Dr. Knud Wümpelmann, general secretary of the European Baptist Federation, says that the European Baptist Convention is one of the greatest supporters of the EBF budget. It gives 6 percent of all undesignated offerings to the Federation and 4 percent to the seminary in Ruschlikon.

The first English-language Baptist church on the continent of Europe was organized as a mission in Frankfurt, Germany, in 1956. Most of the churches have been brought into being without any intervention of the Foreign Mission Board. They are the product of Baptist people living abroad who want churches for themselves and others.

The churches are racially integrated. One of the ushers in a church several years ago was a black man named White. Blacks have served as pastors of predominantly white churches. Race does not enter into church membership or officeholding.

In 1958 the Southern Baptist Convention asked its Foreign Mission Board "to continue to expand its efforts to establish churches for English-speaking people in major cities in countries served by the Foreign Mission Board." The resolution included the statement that "these churches, once established, should, of course, be placed on a self-supporting basis as soon as possible." The Foreign Mission Board decided to appoint missionaries for some English-language churches and asked that such churches relate themselves to Baptist entities in countries where they are located rather than to denominational bodies in the United States.

In 1961 the Foreign Mission Board appointed the first couple for English-language work in Europe. Twenty-one years later forty-four missionaries in Europe were working primarily with Americans living abroad. Most of the churches either have pastors whom they have called from America or lay pastors whose church work is an extra, voluntary responsibility.

The membership of English-language Baptist churches abroad changes frequently. It has been said that "a farewell fellowship hour is a regular monthly activity on the calendar of many churches." A missionary said, "We have to gain 2,000 members every year in the European Baptist Convention just to stay even." When half of a church's members are transferred at one time, it takes faith to believe that others will take their places. Some churches serve their day and go out of existence, such as those in Luxembourg and Iceland; others have a continuing ministry.

Whether permanent or temporary, English-language Baptist churches abroad render a valuable service to the kingdom of God. They minister to some of the many people living away from home, and they strengthen the Baptist witness in lands where they are located.

Scandinavian Baptists

The great Baptist pioneer in *Denmark* was Julius Köbner, who has already been mentioned as one of the associates of Oncken in Germany. Nowhere else do Baptists owe so much to a person of Jewish origin. When Köbner visited Denmark from Hamburg, Germany, he was well received by Lutheran Pietists, some of whom had already independently moved close to the Baptist position. He and Oncken led in the organization of a Baptist church in Copenhagen in 1839. Other churches soon followed in spite of severe repression for about ten years. American (Northern) Baptists helped Denmark, first through the Germany Mission and later directly.

From 1865 to 1879 Köbner lived in Denmark. He built up churches, translated and wrote many hymns, and organized Danish Baptist conferences for studying theology, church polity, and Christian practice. Perhaps because of the tradition he established, Danish Baptists have never suffered from extremes of theology or church practice.

The village of Töllöse, near Copenhagen, is an educational center for Danish Baptists. A "folk high school"—a distinctive Scandinavian development—gives six-month courses, without examinations, to young people after they have ended their formal studies. The emphasis is on personality and character training, religion, Danish culture, and the development of skills. Related to this institution are a "continuation school," with courses lasting ten months, and a more conventional high school. The schools, which enroll up to 220 students, 150 of them boarders, receive state aid. This is not true of the seminary, also located in Töllöse, which dedicated a new building in 1969. Both Southern Baptists and American Baptists made substantial contributions for the seminary building. The enrollment of the seminary, as of several others in Europe, does not normally exceed six or eight.

In 1981 there were forty-two Baptist churches in Denmark, with 6,400 members. They formed the largest free church denomination in the country. However, Baptists in Denmark, as well as the other Scandinavian countries, were declining in membership.

The first Baptist church in *Sweden* was organized in 1848 after a sailor was converted in America and baptized in Hamburg, Germany. A Danish Baptist minister aided in the church organization.

As in Denmark, and also Finland and Norway, Baptist growth took place mainly among Pietists. One of the distinguished Baptist pioneers was Anders Wiberg, who as a Lutheran minister had objected to the superficiality and coldness of his church and left the ministry. Desiring to refute Baptist teaching on baptism, he discussed the subject with Oncken and Köbner and read widely. When his book appeared, it was a defense of believer's baptism. He was baptized, went to America for three years, and then from 1855 until his death in 1887 was the acknowledged leader of Swedish Baptists.

Another great name among Swedish Baptists was Knut O. Broady, who had been a colonel in the American Civil War. He was rector of Bethel Seminary in Stockholm, the first Baptist seminary on the European "mainland," from its founding in 1866 until 1906, and a teacher until 1922. Baptists of England and America helped to pay for the property. (In the 1960s Swedish Baptists, with a little help from America, began a big expansion of their seminary on a new campus at Bromma, a suburb of Stockholm.)

Some of the first Swedish Baptists saw their children forcibly baptized in the Lutheran church. At least one Baptist was exiled, and others left the country voluntarily to escape oppression. The worst was over by 1858. Eventually non-Lutherans were granted recognition in Sweden, but Baptists did not register as a dissenting group and were counted as members of the state church. Since 1952 they have been free to leave the state church, even without registering as members of a recognized religious body, but most have not bothered to do so. Because the distinguished Baptist Gunner Westin was technically listed as a Lutheran, he was able to serve for many years as professor of church history at the University of Uppsala.

The high point in Swedish Baptist statistics was reached in 1935, when there were 68,150 members. Even before then, Pentecostalism had begun to make inroads among Baptists. Some Baptists became Pentecostals. Baptist churches witnessed speaking in tongues. In the 1930s many churches and parts of churches left the Baptist Union to join the Örebro Mission Society, which some people regarded as semi-Pentecostal. It was conservative theologically, emphasized local church autonomy, and majored on evangelism and missions. In 1981 the Baptist Union had 21,651 members, and the Örebro Mission had almost as many.

Influences from Denmark, Sweden, and America entered into the establishment of Baptists in *Norway*. The first Baptist church was organized in 1860. The British Baptist Missionary Society supported the work for a while, and then assistance came for a number of years from American (Northern) Baptists. However, Norwegian Baptists have never received much help from the outside.

After World War II Southern Baptists joined others in contributing to the purchase of property outside Oslo for a seminary and youth school. In 1978 a new building for the seminary, with space also for the Norwegian Baptist Union, was dedicated. In 1970 Southern Baptist assistance, to be given on a diminishing scale for five years, helped Norwegian Baptists to employ their first secretary of evangelism, Günter Wieske, a German married to a Norwegian. His work included directing special conferences and courses, planning campaigns, publishing literature for training in evangelism, and leading a Norwegian Baptist committee on evangelism. He later returned to Germany to lead German Baptist evangelistic work.

Norwegian Baptists numbered 6,299 in 1981. A few years earlier there were 8,000. However, in 1981 a Norwegian

Baptist leader indicated that the tide was changing: "Our Baptist life in Norway is in a period of optimism and progress. We have more young people in our churches than we have had for at least forty years."

Norway has the distinction of having furnished two general secretaries of the Baptist World Alliance. Arnold Ohrn had been director of the Norwegian Baptist Seminary. Josef Nordenhaug had become an American citizen after getting his university education in Norway.

Another distinction of Norwegian Baptists, as indeed of all Scandinavian Baptists, is their dedication to foreign missions. Their per capita gifts to missions and their ratio of missionaries to church members put Southern Baptists to shame.

The first Baptist church in *Finland* was organized in 1856 on the island of Föglö, but more significant was the establishment of churches on the mainland at Pietarsaari and Luvia in 1870. Preachers from Sweden evangelized in Finland, and young men went to the Swedish Baptist Seminary to study. Most of the first Baptists were Swedish-speaking.

Finnish-speaking Baptist churches were started in the course of time. When members of these churches met with their Swedish-speaking brethren, everything that was said had to be translated, for the two languages are not related to each other. For many years, two Baptist unions have existed in Finland. In 1981 the Swedish-speaking group had 1,712 church members, and the other had 730. About 92 percent of the population are Finnish-speaking.

The Pentecostal influence among Finnish Baptists has been considerable. When Baptists see the growth of Pentecostal churches, they are tempted to imitate their methods. However, those who want Pentecostalism usually find a Pentecostal church more appealing than a Baptist one.

At different times Finnish Baptists have received financial

assistance from English Baptists and American Baptists. American Baptists and Southern Baptists have jointly helped in the construction of a few church buildings and of seminary buildings, and also with operating expenses of a Finnish-speaking seminary.

Finnish Baptists have requested a Southern Baptist couple to live and work among them. The missionaries will need unusual linguistic ability, for the Finnish language is one of the most difficult languages. They will need great tact in working among the friendly but proud and independent Finnish people. No Baptists in Europe are more isolated by language than those speaking Finnish, or more responsive to genuine expressions of friendship and fellowship.

Interdenominational Relationships

As has been seen, European Baptists began in a hostile environment. Not only were Catholics opposed to them; Protestant opposition also was strong. The attitude of European Protestants toward Baptists has ranged from complete rejection to grudging toleration, and then to acceptance and even appreciation. Baptists are still a small and little-known minority in most countries, but they have nothing to fear from the established Protestant churches.

The first European Baptists could see little good in the Protestant churches from which they emerged. They doubted the Christian sincerity and orthodoxy of pastors and church members. Feeling the urgency of proclaiming salvation through acceptance of God's grace and the exercise of personal faith in Christ, they insisted on a church membership based on experience of salvation and on the baptism of believers only.

European Baptists still proclaim these principles, but most of them would now admit that the gospel can be heard in many non-Baptist churches. They even see some signs of a general movement in other churches toward believer's baptism and purely voluntary church membership. Influential theologians have come close to the traditional Baptist position on these matters. A random survey in Copenhagen in 1964 showed one-fifth of those questioned sympathetic toward believer's baptism, despite the fact that 95 percent of the Danish people are members of the Lutheran Church.

The present crisis of Baptists in European Protestant countries is due partly to the fact that they, like most Baptists in America, do not feel the urge to evangelize active Protestants and have not yet learned very well how, either alone or with those of other churches, to evangelize the irreligious, the agnostics, and the atheists, whose numbers are increasing rapidly. Most Europeans are still considered members of established (or formerly established) churches: Anglican, Lutheran, Presbyterian (called Reformed in some countries), or Catholic. However, the fact that members were baptized as infants gives those churches no exclusive claim to or responsibility for them. They may listen to Baptists more readily than to representatives of the churches which "claim" them. Irreligious persons are usually not readily responsive to a religious outreach, however, and avoid situations where there is such an outreach. Baptists in Europe face a more difficult but also a more important challenge now than they did in the nineteenth century.

A few Baptist bodies in Europe have sought union with similar bodies. Baptists in Germany and the Soviet Union have already combined with other groups, apparently without sacrificing any Baptist distinctives. A number of British churches have both Baptist and Congregationalist members. Most British Baptist churches practice open membership, accepting without baptism those coming from other denominations, but probably 90 percent of the members are baptized as believers by immersion.

Most European Baptists believe they still have a special

message and some emphases which are needed. The witness to believer's baptism provided by the teaching and practice of a whole denomination, for example, is not made redundant by the teaching (usually without the practice) of believer's baptism by a few theologians or by the protest of many against having been baptized as infants.

European Baptists generally welcome cooperation with fellow Christians. Most Baptist Unions are affiliated in some way with national councils of churches. However, in 1970 Dutch Baptists voted against even guest membership in the national council of churches because of "very disappointing experiences at the local level in ecumenical work." In 1969 the Baptist Union of Scotland voted to remain in the Scottish Council of Churches so long as their influence and distinctive doctrinal emphases were not clearly rejected. English Baptists have from the beginning played a leading role in the British Free-Church Council and also in the British Council of Churches. In 1970 Swiss Baptists voted to join a new council of churches, with limited scope, including the Reformed, Roman Catholics, Old Catholics, and Methodists.

Several European Baptist bodies have joined the World Council of Churches. Two later withdrew. In 1981 Baptist unions in Great Britain, Denmark, Hungary, and the Soviet Union held membership in the World Council. Baptist leader Ernest Payne of England was at one time one of the six presidents of the Council.

Full cooperation exists between Baptist bodies in the World Council of Churches and those outside it. Whether in councils of churches or not, most Baptists would probably agree with John Smyth, of the seventeenth century, that "all penitent and faithful Christians are brethren . . . by what name soever they are known."

All European Christians, and those who work with them, face an urgent challenge. One Baptist leader in a Protestant country said: "I do believe that we can and will grow again, but this will not be possible without repentance, without deeper convictions (also in regard to the task of Baptists), and without a new challenging vision of the task which Jesus Christ has given us in our generation. There are people here who are willing."

Building of Moscow Baptist Church; (left to right) Mr. Mitskevich, Mrs. J. D. Hughey, Dr. J. D. Hughey, and Mr. Ilya Orlov.

Choir singing in house church, Orel, Russia.

Pastor Cornel Mara, president of the Baptist Union of Rumania; Pavel Barbatei, general secretary of the Rumanian Baptist Union; missionary John David Hopper.

Rumanian committee meeting in session at the European Baptist Federation Building, Paris.

Baptist Church building, Krakow, Poland.

Baptist Church Building, Heidelberg, Germany. Building is used by both German-speaking and English-speaking congregations.

Dr. and Mrs. Clyde Fant. Dr. Fant is president of Baptist Theological Seminary, Ruschlikon-Zurich, Switzerland.

Pastoral care class, Baptist Theological Seminary, Ruschlikon-Zurich, Switzerland.

Monument of four reformers (left to right) John Calvin, Guillaume Farel, Theodore De Beze, and John Knox, Geneva, Switzerland.

Administration building, Baptist Theological Seminary, Ruschlikon.

Building of First Baptist Church, Madrid, Spain.

Andre Thobois, pastor of Avenue du Main Baptist Church and president of the French Baptist Federation, working in his study at his home in Paris.

Dr. Gerhard Claas, general secretary, Baptist World Alliance.

Isam Ballenger, Foreign Mission Board secretary for Europe and the Middle East and Keith Parker, professor at Baptist Theological Seminary, Ruschlikon.

Italian evangelistic rally. Missionary Stanley Crabb (left) plays the accordion as Pastor Saverio Guarna (right) leads congregational singing.

Knud Wümpelmann, general secretary of the European Baptist Federation, greets Dr. J. D. Hughey.

5/Baptists in Communist Lands

About one third of the people of the world and half of the people of Europe live under Communist governments. And there were no Communist nations before 1917! Approximately two-thirds of the Baptists of Europe, counting the entire Soviet Union, are in Communist-controlled countries.

Communism and Religion

After saying that Communism may be broadly defined as "any social system in which all property is held in common," Henlee Barnette stated: "Communism today is a worldwide conspiracy which seeks to establish a society in which everything is owned and controlled by the government, based upon a materialistic view of all reality derived from the atheistic philosophy of Karl Marx, implemented by the revolutionary tactics of V. I. Lenin, and directed by a small dedicated and dictatorial political party."

Communism is a powerful protest movement against exploitation of the poor and downtrodden. Communism aims at a total restructuring of society and is therefore revolutionary. It holds that the dictatorship of the proletariat (working people) is eventually inevitable and that its arrival can be hastened by those dedicated to its realization. It regards as good anything that contributes to progress toward the goal of a Communist society.

Many sensitive and concerned people have turned to

87

Communism or some other leftist movement. André Gide wrote:

> What brought me to Communism with my whole heart was the fact of the privileged position which I personally enjoy—that seemed to me preposterous and intolerable. . . . I cling tenaciously to the one fact that I cannot accept a place in a lifeboat in which only a limited number of people are saved.

Helmut Gollwitzer described the experience of a young German Marxist convert he met in a prisoner-of-war camp:

> . . . a new world is opened up before him, and at the same time he is shown a way—the way in which these men are fighting for a better world. . . . The disappointed, perplexed, characterless, blasé, self-centered, middle-class youth sees himself invited for the first time to pledge his life for a purpose that has a meaning; the joy of sacrifice and a teaching which satisfies both heart and mind beckon to him. Marxism has become for him a decisive spiritual experience.

Alas, that such a person should be defrauded! There is no inevitable progress for the world. Human nature is not changed simply by changing the structure of society, and sinful man is capable of terrible injustice and selfishness in every kind of society. Communism does not eliminate human suffering. Working people may be exploited under a system of state ownership as well as under other systems.

And what of the methods for overthrowing the old order? Can the elusive goal of a good life for the poor justify deceit and violence? What happens to the character of the revolutionary? Is he not in danger of becoming a criminal in mind and heart? Can devotion to the cause of the poor atone for hatred of the rich or those not quite poor? Does the Communist really love people, or is he just devoted to a system? Are there not better ways to cope with poverty and injustice, to make life better for human beings, and to create a better society?

There is a fundamental ideological conflict between Communism and religion. The official Communist philosophy is dialectical and historical materialism. This means that nature and history are interpreted from a purely materialistic point of view. Development from lower to higher takes place as a consequence of the struggle of opposite tendencies in nature and society. There is no place in the universe for God.

Karl Marx called religion the "opium of the people." Lenin said: "Marxism is materialism. As such it is mercilessly hostile to all religion."

Communism is the greatest threat to Christianity since the rise of Islam 1,360 years ago. Communists hope for the death of all religion. They combat it through education and propaganda, limitation and control, exploitation of weaknesses, disagreements and errors, and, when expedient, the closing of churches and the arrest and punishment of believers. The limits and the duration of toleration in a Communist state will always be uncertain.

Still, religion lives on in Communist countries. There are Baptists in most of them. In some places they have grown strong swimming against the stream; elsewhere their growth has been stunted.

Baptists in a Catholic and Communist Background

About 95 percent of the people of *Poland* are Catholics. They have held fast to their religion through years of independence, rule by Russia, Prussia, and Austria, revival as a nation after World War I, and domination by Communists after World War II. As this is being written a political, economic, and social crisis is revealing remarkable strength in the Catholic Church, and also its vulnerability.

The Catholic Church was too firmly rooted in Polish soil to be pulled up by Communism. The hierarchy has asserted and usually has maintained its independence, and Church influence has been pitted with some success against Communist Party influence. Church activities have been curtailed but are still more extensive than in most other Communist countries. Baptists and other free churchmen apparently were favored for a while as potential allies against Catholicism.

The first Baptists in what is now Poland were of German origin. A church was started near Warsaw in 1858. Other churches of Germans, Czechs, and Poles were formed.

In independent Poland between World Wars I and II, Baptists had new opportunities for development. According to the London agreement of 1920, the American Baptist Foreign Mission Society and the German-speaking Baptists of America gave assistance in Poland. By 1939 there were 17,000 Baptists in the country—7,745 in a Slavic union and the others in a German union.

Great losses were suffered during the war, and at its close most Germans departed. About 2,000 Baptists were left in the country. By 1981 they had increased to 2,545. Marked improvements in education were noted. Most young and middle-aged Baptists had a high-school education. Many held university and school of technology degrees, and several had earned doctorates.

A Baptist from East Germany mentioned in an address to the European Baptist Conference in 1969 that the ten students who had graduated recently from the Polish Baptist Seminary would all earn their living in secular work but would still be preachers. One would go back to the woods as a forester, another to a factory, and another to an office. The speaker said: "Nobody will fear such a man, because he has no special position, and no one will envy him, for he is not so well off. How hard it is for us to lead men to Christ when they fear or envy us!"

Some financial assistance from abroad has gone to Polish Baptists. The construction of a beautiful church, a seminary, and a Baptist headquarters building in Warsaw gave Baptists of many nations an opportunity to help. The Southern Baptist Foreign Mission Board and the American Baptist Foreign Mission Society gave substantial amounts; and most of the Baptist groups of Europe and some in other continents had a part in the building. The most sacrificial giving was done by Polish Baptists. The dedication of the building in 1961 was a time of international rejoicing.

In the early 1980s Baptists of other countries mounted a massive relief effort for Poland. Southern Baptists and European Baptists pooled their resources to give food, clothing, and medicines to Baptists and others of Poland. Seldom has more joy in giving been noted.

The *Hungarians* became Catholics about AD 1000. During the Reformation, two-thirds of them turned to Protestantism, but Roman Catholicism soon regained its hold on most of the people. During the latter part of the nineteenth century, religious liberty was instituted.

Baptists first appeared in Hungary in the 1840s. The first permanent church was started in 1874. At about that time Heinrich Meyer of Germany began his remarkable missionary career of over forty years. A man of considerable ability, he traveled over Hungary preaching and organizing groups of believers. Strange to say, however, he never learned the Hungarian language (the second language of the Austro-Hungarian Empire), and he wanted all churches to be branches of his church in Budapest.

By the turn of the century Hungarian-speaking Baptists, led by Andras Udvarnoki, began to assert their independence. Several churches organized a Baptist union, which applied for and received recognition by the government, with the right to own property. When recognition was denied Meyer's churches, they declared the seeking of governmental recognition to be unbaptistic. Representatives of the Baptist World Alliance helped the two groups to become reconciled and form one Baptist union.

By the time of World War I there were approximately twenty thousand Baptists in Hungary. The breakup of the empire left only about a third as many in the new nation of Hungary. In 1921 Southern Baptists, following the London Conference of 1920, began to help them. Of particular importance was assistance in acquiring property for a seminary and a girls' training school, which had missionary teachers.

These buildings and also several church buildings were destroyed in World War II. Church life was disrupted. After the war, help was given for new seminary and church property. When the government became Communist, foreign ties ceased for several years. Church activities were closely supervised by the authorities, and a number of pastors were removed from office. However, churches remained open, and the seminary was allowed to function with a small enrollment. Limited financial assistance from Southern Baptists was again possible by the 1960s. There were about twelve thousand six hundred members of Hungarian Baptist churches in 1981.

In the late 1970s and early 1980s Hungarian Baptists received permission to build a number of churches. They gave sacrificially of their money (20 percent of the family income in many instances) and of their time (most of the work was done by volunteers) to make the buildings possible. Southern Baptists joined other foreign Baptist groups in funding the building projects. Yet funds always lagged behind needs!

In 1969 a Hungarian Protestant leader, Zoltam Kaldy, gave a significant address on "The Situation of the Church in the Socialist Society." He stated that in the new social order born out of the revolution following World War II, the churches faced and rejected four options: (1) the way of opposition or resistance, which would have been required if the state had demanded denial of faith in Christ or of the obligation to love one's neighbors; (2) the way of conformism, which would have meant being identified with Marxism and using the gospel to buttress it; (3) going into the ghetto, separating from society; (4) trying to recapture the former positions of power. Hungarian churches refused those alternatives and chose the way of diaconia. This means unselfish service linked with the preaching of the Word. Kaldy said:

> It belongs to the way of the diaconia that with a clear distinction between gospel and ideology, we seek out those areas of social life in which, with good conscience bound to the Word of God, we may cooperate with men of other world views for the good of man. . . .
>
> I want to voice our thanks to God for the fact that we, led by the Word of God, have found our place and service in one new Hungarian world.

The sentiment of many Hungarian Baptists was similar. They did not oppose the social and political order, nor did they sacrifice what they regarded as essentials of their Christian faith and practice. Communists and Christians in Hungary have learned to live side by side and to cooperate.

Czechoslovakia is about 75 percent Roman Catholic, but, as the home of John Hus and a focal point of the Protestant Reformation, it has a long tradition of religious dissent. As an independent republic between the two world wars it became a remarkably free and progressive country.

Baptists first appeared in what is now Czechoslovakia (then included in Austria-Hungary) as a part of the German Baptist movement. In 1885 a Czech church was organized. When a Czechoslovak Baptist Union was formed in 1919 it included Czech, Slovak, German, and Hungarian churches (twenty-five in all). In the London Conference of 1920 it was decided that Northern (American) Baptists, British Baptists, and others would give assistance.

After Communists took control of the government in 1948, religious freedom was guaranteed by the constitution, but all clergymen were required to take an oath of loyalty to the government and were paid by the state. Being government employees was a new experience for Baptist pastors! Thirteen Baptist pastors were imprisoned for several years on the charge of being American spies.

The brief liberalization of the Communist government in 1968 brought new religious freedom. Baptists reported that children could be trained at church, a youth organization had been started, and ministers who had been deprived of the right to preach could again preach. Plans were made for reorganizing and expanding the work.

Freedom was short-lived. Through Russian power, Czechoslovakia was brought back to the "straight and narrow" road of Communism. This brought restrictions on church life and uncertainty as to the future extent of toleration. Baptist church membership in 1981 was 3,982.

Rumania, Yugoslavia, and Bulgaria

Rumania and Bulgaria are Eastern Orthodox countries. Yugoslavia is Orthodox, Roman Catholic, and Muslim. Much of the Orthodox world has fallen under the control of Communism. The only Orthodox countries that have stayed out of the Communist orbit are Greece and Cyprus. This does not mean that Orthodoxy and Communism have a special attraction. It means that Eastern Europe, where Orthodoxy prevails, has fallen under Communist rule.

German Baptist influence reached *Rumania* in the 1850s. In the part of Hungary that was added to Rumania after

World War I, Heinrich Meyer, stationed in Budapest, was active from 1873. More growth took place there than in the "Old Kingdom." In the entire nation of Rumania there were about seventeen thousand Baptists in 1920. They belonged to Rumanian, Hungarian, German, and Russian elements of the population. The 1920 London agreement made Southern Baptists responsible for helping the Baptist cause in Rumania.

In spite of the fact that the Versailles Treaty guaranteed religious freedom for minorities, severe persecution broke out in the new territories. Rumanians were supposed to be loyal members of the Rumanian Orthodox Church! Baptist chapels were closed, meetings were broken up, preachers and others were attacked and imprisoned, property was seized, and burials were interfered with. J. H. Rushbrooke, the general secretary of the Baptist World Alliance, made repeated visits to Rumania to intercede with the king, the prime minister, and other government officials on behalf of Baptists. Petitions went to the Rumanian government from many countries. Just before World War II, the Baptist World Alliance expressed satisfaction that churches closed the preceding year had been reopened and hope that full religious freedom would be established.

Southern Baptists' main contribution to Rumania was in the field of education. They bought property for and operated a seminary and a girls' training school. Southern Baptists' and Rumanian Baptists' disagreement over the administration of the schools closed them for a while. There was also some disunity among Rumanian Baptists. Still, remarkable growth took place.

World War II and the establishment afterwards of a Communist government ended Southern Baptist participation in the work. Rumanian Baptists became one of the most isolated Baptist groups in Europe. Seldom were Rumanians permitted to attend international meetings, and foreigners were not often invited to visit the churches.

In the early 1960s Rumanian Baptists had to reorganize their churches; they lost hundreds of them in the process. Permission for baptisms had to be secured. This was especially difficult if the person to be baptized had been brought up as Orthodox. Enrollment in the seminary, which once went to ninety, averaged six to ten students. The seminary was closed for a short time. Church services usually were permitted only on Saturday night and Sunday morning. Good use was made of limited freedom. Church services were long, and they included Bible instruction.

By the mid-1970s governmental pressures on Baptists were declining. Some Christian literature could be legally imported and/or printed in the country. A larger seminary enrollment was permitted. The number of authorized church services increased. Baptisms were more freely authorized. Several church buildings could be constructed.

An earthquake damaged one of the two seminary buildings in 1977. An urban development plan has nullified efforts to obtain permission to put up a new building, and funds provided by the Foreign Mission Board were redesignated for needs elsewhere. Seminary classes are small.

Rumanian Baptists are the fastest-growing Baptist group in Europe, and one of the fastest growing in the world. By 1981 official statistics were showing 160,000 members of the churches. Approximately 20,000 new converts were being baptized each year.

Yugoslavia is another nation created after World War I. It became Communist after World War II, but it successfully declared its independence of Moscow and usually has permitted more religious and civil freedom than the other Communist countries have permitted. A Yugoslav once laughingly said to the writer: "This is the Tito Bridge. Sometimes it leans to the West and sometimes to the East." Any leaning to the West has usually meant more freedom.

When Yugoslavia came into being there were about six hundred Baptists in the old Hungarian territory (mainly Catholic). There had been a few in the Serbia section, which is Serbian Orthodox; but they were scattered by 1918. Yugoslavia became one of the new mission fields of Southern Baptists after the London Conference of 1920. This was a country in which religious toleration was generous.

Vincent Vacek, who belonged to a Croatian Catholic family of Czech origin but was converted in America after moving there, was sent by the Southern Baptist Foreign Mission Board to Yugoslavia as a national missionary. A zealous and tireless evangelist, he had the satisfaction of seeing Baptists increase to 2,395 before his death in 1939. He led the five language groups of Baptists to organize their own conventions, with all united in a national Baptist union.

Just before Vacek's death, John Allen Moore and Mrs. Moore arrived to begin missionary service in Yugoslavia. They opened a small seminary, but the outbreak of war soon caused it to close and the missionaries to leave. Except for a few months, the Communist government did not permit the Moores to live in Yugoslavia, but they visited there regularly through the years.

In the 1970s the Southern Baptist missionaries, Dr. and Mrs. James A. Williams, Jr., were able to establish missionary residence in Yugoslavia by virtue of her dual citizenship, and she continued her work there after his death in an accident in 1981.

Some financial assistance from the Foreign Mission Board has gone annually to Yugoslav Baptist work.

Southern Baptists and many other groups contributed to the cost of large and attractive buildings for the Baptist seminary and the church in Novi Sad. The dedication took place in 1967. It is significant that a Communist government would permit such construction. Even the need of foreign exchange would not have been sufficient motivation if there had been a strong conviction that Baptist life should be, and could be, snuffed out.

Yugoslav Baptists have Sunday Schools, women's organizations, and youth conventions. No churches have been closed by the authorities. There has been no serious attempt to infiltrate or control the Baptist Union. However, mass evangelism outside churches and the use of the mass media (except for radio broadcasts from outside the country by Yugoslav citizens) are impossible. In 1981 Yugoslav Baptists numbered 3,510. A slight decline in the last few years is attributed to the emigration of large numbers of people.

The Baptist Seminary in Yugoslavia admits university students who follow two programs of study at the same time. It is hoped that this will raise the general level of education in the churches and pulpits and will also encourage the development of a bivocational ministry, with pastors, especially of small churches, earning their livelihood in secular vocations.

Bulgaria, an Eastern Orthodox country with a Muslim minority, came under Communist rule after World War II. Baptist origins there go back to the 1880s and the influence of Russians, especially persons of German origin. German Baptists of America gave some assistance for a number of years. Growth has been very slow; losses have occurred since World War II; and in 1981 there were only 650 Baptists in the country.

Religious freedom has been severely limited in Bulgaria. Baptists have been politically suspect, and they have feared the consequences of contacts with persons from the West.

The Soviet Union

Russia has the distinction of being the first country to establish a Marxist-Communist government and social order and one of the first to espouse atheism officially. Throughout history most governments have been friendly toward religion, or at least toward one religion; but the Soviet Union blazed a trail for official atheism and for a policy aimed at the elimination of religion. The policy has been followed with variations of intensity and strategy.

Russia has the largest Eastern Orthodox population in the world. Moscow was thought of by many Russians as "the third Rome," the successor of Rome and Constantinople in Christian and political leadership of the world. There was a close union of church and state in czarist times. The czars were described in Russian Orthodox catechisms as "the chief guardians and protectors of the Church." The czar appointed members of the holy synod, which governed the church, and the high procurator, who controlled the synod. The Orthodox Church was financially and morally supported by the state and was in turn the chief bulwark of the state. The situation has changed completely since 1917, but Orthodoxy is still the religion of the majority of Russians who are religious.

There are more Baptists in the Soviet Union than in any other country except the United States and India. Exactly how many Baptists are in the Soviet Union is difficult to say. For a number of years the official figure has been 545,000. Foreign estimates of the total number of Baptists, registered and nonregistered, run as high as three or four million, but these estimates are probably excessive.

Russian Baptists got started in czarist times. Nikita Voronin, of Tiflis in the Caucasus, was baptized by a German in 1867. Other people were converted and baptized, and a Baptist movement in the Caucasus began. Even before this, Stundism (so called because of the German word *Stunde,* meaning "hour," since people gathered for hours of prayer and Bible reading) had started in the Ukraine among Germans and then Russians. Beginning in the 1870s a Baptist movement, known as Evangelical Christian, began in St. Petersburg with the preaching of

Lord Radstock from England and the conversion first of some socially prominent people, followed by other Russians. Representatives of the different groups met in St. Petersburg in 1884, but before they could accomplish much police ordered the conference closed. Some of the participants were arrested. The Russian Baptist Union and the Evangelical Christian Union were both members of the Baptist World Alliance.

The rapid growth of Baptists and Evangelical Christians alarmed the Orthodox Church and the Russian government. The high procurator said, "Russia . . . will never allow that the Orthodox Church's children should be taken away from her and enrolled in alien flocks." Many "heretics" were fined, flogged, imprisoned, and exiled. Vasily Pavloff, long a leader of Russian Baptists, told the Baptist World Alliance in 1905 that when he returned from his first exile in Siberia the police demanded of him a pledge that he would not preach again. He answered: "I will not give you that. Do you think I am frightened? I will preach." He was again banished to Siberia for his courageous stand.

Baptists and Evangelical Christian groups were reported to number 106,000 in 1914, less than fifty years after the first Baptist baptism.

The revolution temporarily brought more freedom for Russian Baptists. The first "religious task" of the Communists was to break the power of the Orthodox Church. The reactionary position of many of the clergy added fuel to the flames. For about twelve years Baptists and Evangelical Christians attracted little attention and were permitted a large amount of freedom. The 1918 constitution of the Russian Republic stated: "With the object of securing real freedom of conscience for the workers, the church is separated from the state, and the school from the church, but freedom of religious and antireligious propaganda is recognized for all citizens."

A Russian delegate to the Baptist World Congress of 1928 reported two hundred thousand church members and made the following statement about conditions in his country:

> The constitution of our country decrees and realizes in practice the complete separation of the church from the state. . . . Further, in accordance with the Constitution of the Soviet Republic, every citizen can propagate any religion. Religious freedom and antireligious propaganda is the right of all citizens. . . . We have the full right to hold meetings and teach in them the Word of God, and our evangelistic work has already spread beyond the confines of the Russian people and is gradually spreading among the heathens and Mohammedans living in our country. Further, we have the possibility of publishing our periodicals . . . and the books of Holy Scripture, and also received in 1927 the official authority to open in Moscow a Preachers' School.

The situation changed in 1929. Stalin cracked down on all kinds of freedom. The article on religion in the constitution of the Russian Republic was changed to read: "Freedom in the exercise of religious worship and freedom of anti-religious propaganda is recognized for all citizens." This statement is incorporated in the present U.S.S.R. constitution. Churches are therefore limited by the basic law of the nation to worship and, by implication at least, are denied the right to make their beliefs and practices public. Antireligious propaganda was intensified in 1929, and Baptists were singled out for special attack.

A 1929 "Law on Religious Associations," supplemented by instructions from government authorities, subjected the churches to close supervision and control and severely limited religious activities. As a matter of fact, these laws, still in effect, contradicted the constitutional guarantee of freedom of worship.

Every "religious association" was required to apply for registration before holding meetings. Many churches remained unregistered because they got no reply to their applications for registration, or because they were passed from office to office. The names of church members had to be supplied. The authorities were given the power to remove members from the executive body of a religious association. Churches were forbidden to form mutual aid associations; to organize special meetings for children, young people, or women; to have special groups for the teaching of religion; or to maintain libraries or reading rooms. The religious education of children was banned except by parents in the home, and the right of parents was not made explicit. Baptists and Evangelical Christians lost their theological schools, their magazines, their right to print the Bible, their special services for children, and their right to engage in general evangelistic activities. Many church leaders were deprived of food cards as nonlaboring persons, were imprisoned, or were exiled. And many churches were closed.

World War II brought a change in the religious situation. The Russian Orthodox Church, after a great show of loyalty to the government, was permitted to reorganize with the patriarch at its head and to open several seminaries for the training of priests. The Baptists and Evangelical Christians were permitted to hold a small conference in 1944 in which it was agreed to unite the two groups. They also declared their loyalty to the government and even stated repeatedly to foreigners that they enjoyed religious freedom, perhaps meaning simply that they had more freedom than formerly. The Orthodox Church and the Baptists began publishing journals. They could also bring out limited editions of the Bible and, for the Baptists, a hymnal. Churches—only one Baptist church in Moscow, for example, and one in Leningrad—were crowded with worshipers. Sunday Schools were still not permitted, nor was there freedom to deal with social and political questions.

In 1954 the Central Committee of the Communist Party issued a decree signed by Krushchev "On Mistakes in the Conduct of Scientific Atheist Propaganda." It insisted that everything possible be done to free men from "religious prejudices" but that there be no direct attacks on churches or individuals:

> In accordance with its programme, the Communist Party is carrying on propaganda of scientific enlightenment in the materialist outlook, aimed at constantly raising the consciousness of the working masses and gradually freeing them from religious prejudices . . . at the same time the party has always considered it essential to avoid causing any offence to the feelings of believers. . . . It is imperative to bear in mind that offensive actions with regard to the church, to the clergy, or to believing citizens are incompatible with the line adopted by the Party and the State in the conduct of scientific atheist propaganda, and are in contradiction to the USSR Constitution, which provides freedom of conscience to Soviet citizens.

The attack on religion became more direct within a few years. In a speech to the Communist Party Congress in 1961 Krushchev demanded greater attention to measures against religion. The Russian Orthodox Church was reorganized so that control of local churches passed to purged "councils of twenty" in the parishes. It is estimated that ten thousand Orthodox churches, about half of the total, were closed in the space of a few years. District committees were set up to supervise religious communities, to discover unregistered groups, to collect and analyze data on attendance at religious services, to study methods used by ministers and churches, especially for influencing youth and children, and to discover ways of limiting and weakening activities of religious groups. Of eight Orthodox seminaries existing in 1958, only three were left in 1965.

Many Baptist churches were closed. There was a ready

pretext—they were not registered. A group of Baptists stated
in a letter to Krushchev in 1963:

> Registration of ECB [Evangelical Christian Baptist]
> churches was accepted for only two years (1947-48). During
> this time only a small proportion of churches were registered
> and they were turned into a special showcase for freedom of
> conscience. Behind this, the majority of churches were left
> without any rights and in spite of repeated appeals they
> remained unregistered. Obviously this was so that at any
> time they could be classified as illegal and subjected to
> persecution, with the purpose of liquidating them.

Signers of the petition were leaders of the "Organizing
Committee of the Evangelical Christian Baptist Church."
They were a part of a dissident Baptist movement that
appeared in 1961. Known as the Initiative Group or Action
Group, they set up an organizing committee and eventually
a Council of Churches of the Evangelical Christians and
Baptists, which was intended to replace the All-Union
Council of Evangelical Christians-Baptists. Estimates of their
strength vary from twelve thousand to one hundred thou-
sand.

The occasion for the Baptist schism was the issuance in
1960 of New Statutes for the All-Union Council of Evangelical Christians-Baptists and of a Letter of Instructions to the
Churches from the All-Union Council. Both documents
were concessions to the stricter Soviet policy on religion.
The statutes called for stricter control of congregations by
the central body. Probably especially difficult for the
churches were the statements that services could be held
only in places of worship provided by the state or in suitable
rented quarters and never (except for funerals) in private
dwellings, for many groups had tried and failed to obtain
church buildings and were limited to private dwellings for
their services. According to accusations brought by the
Initiative Group, the All-Union Council discouraged evange-

lism, the baptism of persons under thirty, and the attendance of children at church services.

The dissident Baptists demanded of the All-Union Council of Evangelical Christians-Baptists that a general Baptist convention be called. Failing to get the response they desired, they tried without success to obtain from Soviet authorities permission to hold a Baptist convention. Leaders of the All-Union Council were declared excommunicated by the dissident group. The All-Union Council has held several conventions since then, but with little representation of the dissidents, partly because many of the leaders were in prison and partly because the breach between the two Baptist groups had become too wide. However, the statutes were modified to remove some of the things that had been so objectionable to the dissidents, and apparently the 1961 Letter of Instructions was withdrawn. The theme of the 1969 convention, "That they may be one," suggested the earnest desire of Baptist leaders for unity.

On a tour of the Soviet Union in 1970, John Allen Moore was told by a member of the All-Union Council: "We feel brotherly love toward these people, and sympathy for them in their sufferings. We have sent appeals to the authorities that they be dealt with leniently. But they anathematize us because we obey our country's laws and because of our membership in the World Council of Churches. We remain ready to welcome them back into the churches, and thousands have returned."

The sufferings of the dissidents were real. They openly disobeyed the laws on religion and were arrested. The Soviet press reported many of these incidents. Baptists had more publicity than they had ever had before. Petitions went from the group to Soviet authorities and eventually to the United Nations, the Baptist World Alliance, and other foreign agencies. Relatives of imprisoned persons held a conference and organized to publicize their plight. They declared that the total number of Evangelical Christians-Baptists sentenced for their religious activity between 1961 and June 1964 was 197. The number increased after that. A carefully prepared list of prisoners was made public. The most common sentence was for three years, but several persons were given five or even ten years.

In May, 1966, a delegation of about five hundred Initiative Baptists from many parts of the Soviet Union went to Moscow to seek an interview with Brezhnev, the head of the Communist Party. They bore a letter asking for permission to hold a congress, recognition of their organization, freedom of those imprisoned for their faith, the end of state interference in church life, and freedom of religious instruction. After they had waited through a day and night, ten of their number were admitted for an audience. The others began to hold a prayer meeting in the street, to the amazement of passersby, but they were soon roughly crowded into buses by policemen. The prayer meeting continued in the courtyard of the police station. Some of the group were set free the next day; others were kept in prison ten or fifteen days.

Late in 1969 the newspaper *Izvestia* carried an article by the chairman of the government's Council for Religious Affairs stating that the Initiative Baptists were "trying to stop believers from registering their organization with state organs, and frightening regular Baptists by telling them that registration of religious organizations leads straight to hell." Such activity, he said, is against Soviet law and those engaging in it were being brought to order by the courts. The dissident Baptists must cease their provocative activities. Since then, reports have indicated that Initiative Baptists were registering their churches and that their difficulties with the authorities were diminishing.

Signs of greater freedom in the Soviet Union began to appear in the late 1960s. Perhaps both the protests of the dissidents and the diplomacy of All-Union Council Baptists had some influence on developments. The All-Union Council received permission to conduct a correspondence course for one hundred persons. Mimeographed materials on the Bible, theology, homiletics, pastoral theology, church history, and the Soviet constitution are mailed out once a month to the pastors and would-be pastors who are enrolled; written assignments are graded; and twice a year all of the students assemble for examinations. This is highly significant, since for nearly forty years there was no formal ministerial training for Baptists in Russia.

Limited editions of the Bible and a hymnal have been permitted, as have several foreign shipments of Bibles. In 1980, Alexei Bichkov, general secretary of the All-Union Council of Evangelical Christians-Baptists, said he thought every Baptist family in the Soviet Union had a Bible. Thirteen new churches in the Moscow area, twelve to a hundred miles from the city, have been authorized.

After his 1970 trip to the Soviet Union, John Allen Moore wrote:

> Church members take seriously their responsibilities as Christians. They witness by their lives daily at the workbench in factories and offices where they work. The long lists of inactive church members so common in our land and others are apparently unknown to Baptist churches in USSR. . . .
>
> Active church people would not [often] be able to attain high position in secular work, for all firms are state-owned, and the government is of course strongly atheistic, ultimately opposed to all religion. . . .
>
> Believers . . . can get respectable jobs and generally they are appreciated for their good work. They can live their faith and they have numerous opportunities to witness to it; they do not worry unduly about those they do not have, nor are they envious of nonbelievers who may attain higher positions.

When my wife and I visited the Soviet Union in the summer of 1979, we were reminded by the confiscation of eight Russian Bibles at the border that religious freedom is still quite limited. However, we were encouraged by the large, enthusiastic congregations in the churches. What a thrill to preach to 2,100 people in Moscow!

In the fall of 1981, Reverend Andreij E. Klimenko, president of the All-Union Council of Evangelical Christians-Baptists, gave an interview in which he said:

> The youth element in services and in churches is growing more and more. This is especially true in regions with a German-speaking population, where youth makes up about half those who attend. They participate actively and in various ways in the meetings—singing, playing instruments, declaiming, and preaching. Occasionally young people take responsibility for an entire service . . .
>
> Just now we are building many new church structures. No less than one hundred new or restored buildings have been erected in this recent period. Several of these are large and well-equipped, such as at Rostov and other places.
>
> As to plans for constructing a pastor's seminary in Moscow, we have just handed in drawings and detailed cost estimates to the authorities. . . . The matter of pastoral education is becoming more and more important. The present correspondence courses are not sufficient. . . .
>
> Our work is blessed in many ways, and we are deeply grateful for that. Besides many conversions and baptisms, we see a deepening fellowship in our Union. Even our brethren who formerly placed themselves outside our fellowship and who have not registered with the authorities are starting to rethink their position.

Rev. Alexei Bichkov, in his report to the forty-second All-Union Congress of Evangelical Christians-Baptists in the USSR in 1979, said:

> We believe that though the combination of socialism and atheism is historical by its nature, it is by no means absolutely

necessary. Such an opinion is shared not only by Christians but also by many progressive individuals and movements that struggle for peace and justice. Historical Christian churches in the past were closely linked to unjust social structures that contributed, to some extent, to negative attitudes towards them under new conditions. But now millions of Christians live in Socialist countries and take active part in the development of their societies. They reflect in their life the eternally living teaching of Jesus Christ which is absolutely independent of any historical conditions. . . .

Our hope that the present and the future of the church is in the hands of Jesus Christ saves us from dependence on the ideological superstructure of our society. We take equal part in the work for the benefit of our neighbors and the society as a whole. We rejoice over its achievements and take its difficulties as our own. We consider ourselves to be an integral part of the society. . . .

In the course of history God has used not only Christians but also secular movements and ideological doctrines, though they have not suspected it, so that humankind can approach the goals of His Kingdom of love and justice.

In Communist countries one hears much in sermon and song about the resurrection. The faith persists that if God could raise Jesus from the dead, he can raise up his church in our world today, protect it, and use it for his glory. This is happening in eastern Europe.

What Can We Do?

Southern Baptists have a very meaningful relationship with the Baptists of eastern Europe. Especially dear are the long-standing ties with the Baptists of Yugoslavia, Hungary, and Rumania; but deeply meaningful also are our relationships with other Baptists throughout eastern Europe.

In a few countries it is possible for the Foreign Mission Board to give regular financial assistance for buildings and even for current expenses of Baptist work. Elsewhere financial help is not needed or cannot be received without embarrassment. Help in such places is limited to prayer, encouragement, occasional visits for preaching or teaching, and strengthening the sense of international brotherhood and fellowship. Those who visit eastern Europe invariably learn more about faith and faithfulness, preaching and personal witnessing, zeal and service.

In 1966 Dr. John Allen Moore became Southern Baptists' fraternal representative to the Baptists of eastern Europe, with the responsibility of cultivating relationships with them through correspondence and visits and of evaluating for the Foreign Mission Board any requests that might come for financial assistance. Three years later he also became the Foreign Mission Board's field representative for Europe.

When Moore retired in 1978 his successor as fraternal representative to the Baptists of eastern Europe was Dr. John David Hopper, who continued to live with his family in Austria. The Hoppers and another couple assigned to Europe became the Southern Baptist mission to eastern Europe, with the expectation that at least one other couple would eventually be appointed. Hopper's services as preacher, teacher, counselor, and friend are in great demand all over eastern Europe. It is amazing how much foreign Christians can do legally for their friends in eastern Europe and how much they can receive and pass on to friends who live elsewhere.

One of the services of our mission to eastern Europe is to make clear that there are Baptists—many of them—in that part of the world who are not "underground."

6/An International Approach in Missions

Europe is witnessing the development of an international approach in missions. Of course, foreign missions is by its very nature international: The Christians of one country witness for Christ in another and help fellow believers there fulfill their Christian mission. Mission strategy has generally concentrated on particular countries. This will doubtless continue. However, some efforts are directed toward more than one country at the same time and are, therefore, quite international in character.

Growth of Internationalism

The international approach is in step with the times. Certainly, travel has never been so easy or so common, nor has it ever been so easy for people in different lands to communicate with one another. Businesses compete on a worldwide scale. Businessmen travel from country to country. Though there are walls that separate nations from one another, no nation can really isolate itself from the rest of the world. There are organizations that attempt an international approach in dealing with world problems.

The Roman Empire once provided political unity in the Mediterranean world and northward through Europe as far as England. Trading and cultural exchange flourished. After the Germanic invasions, however, Europe was fragmented. People settled down within the walls of castles and cities and behind geographical barriers such as rivers and mountains.

Cultural and linguistic differences and geographically re-
stricted loyalties developed. Still, there was a certain unity in
Europe—the unity of Christendom. The Roman Popes
claimed temporal powers much as the Caesars did. Even
when these could not be asserted, the papacy had great
"spiritual" powers, for the period of the Middle Ages was a
time of faith and superstition. Roman Catholic faith and
practice bound western Europe together.

With the growth of modern nation states, men began to
think of themselves as Englishmen, Frenchmen, or Spaniards. National interests frequently clashed; ambitions and
rivalries led to war. The first half of the twentieth century
witnessed two world wars that started in Europe.

After World War I, the desire for world peace and unity
led to the creation of the League of Nations. It failed because
nations were unwilling to surrender any of their sovereignty
and because the United States did not join (though the
American President was chiefly responsible for creating it).

World War II was followed by the creation of the United
Nations. Like the League of Nations, it often proves impo-
tent because of national rivalries and power plays, but it
does provide an international forum for the discussion of
problems and an international apparatus for dealing with
some of them.

Since Europeans have suffered much from rivalries and
wars between nations, they have been especially active in
the search for unity. The European Economic Community
or Common Market is the most important expression of
European internationalism. The Council of Europe, with its
committee of ministers representing governments and its
parliament representing national parliaments, has passed
influential resolutions and made significant recommenda-
tions on economic, cultural, social, political, and legal
matters. Other expressions of internationalism include the
North Atlantic Treaty Organization (NATO), the Warsaw

Pact, and the European Free Trade Association.

The welfare of men and nations calls for unity. As one chief of state said after World War II, "It is certain that unless we learn to live together we shall all die together."

Baptist Internationalism

Baptists of the world have found ways of promoting international fellowship and cooperation. For many years they dreamed of a worldwide Baptist organization. Their dream became a reality in 1905 when representatives of twenty-three countries met in London for the first Baptist World Congress. The Baptist World Alliance, composed of national Baptist bodies, came into being at that time. The preamble to the constitution states:

> The Baptist World Alliance, extending over every part of the world, exists in order more fully to show the essential oneness of Baptist people in the Lord Jesus Christ, to impart inspiration to the brotherhood, and to promote the spirit of fellowship, service, and cooperation among its members; but this alliance may in no way interfere with the independence of the churches or assume the administrative functions of existing organizations.

The sense of unity among European Baptists led them to organize European Baptist conferences in Berlin in 1908 and in Stockholm in 1913. Reference has been made to the fact that meetings held in London in 1920 and 1948 under the auspices of the Baptist World Alliance considered postwar problems in Europe and ways Baptists should use their resources.

In 1950 the European Baptist Federation was created. Its constitution sets forth the following purposes:

> To provide fellowship among Baptists in Europe, to stimulate and coordinate evangelism in Europe, to provide a

board of consultation and planning for Baptist mission work
in Europe, to stimulate and coordinate wherever possible the
foreign mission work of European Baptists who have no field
of their own, to provide such Baptist relief work as may be
needed in Europe.

In order to promote fellowship among Baptists in Europe,
the Federation secretary, who is an associate secretary of the
Baptist World Alliance, visits the various European countries
and maintains correspondence with Baptists in them. European Baptist congresses are held periodically. The Federation Council meets every other year. It includes representation from each Baptist union in Europe and also from
International Ministries of American Baptist Churches in the
U.S.A. and the Southern Baptist Foreign Mission Board. In
alternate years the smaller executive committee meets.
Committees of European Baptist women, youth, and men
promote work among their groups in the various countries
and plan international conferences for them.

The Federation has set up international committees on
Belgium and Austria to promote evangelism and church
work in the two countries. There is also a committee on
Rumania which is responsible for radio broadcasts to that
country, the sending of Bibles, and attention to other needs.
In 1967 the Federaton appointed an evangelism committee
because of widespread interest in simultaneous evangelism.
It was later combined with a committee on Christian
education, and the joint committee plans and conducts
periodic conferences on evangelism and education.

Closely related to the Federation, but independent of it, is
the European Baptist Mission. Supported by Baptists of
European countries who do not have their own foreign
mission channels, the society maintains about a hundred
missionaries in Cameroon, Sierra Leone, Argentina, Brazil,
Peru, and Portugal. Members of the European Baptist
Mission are Baptist unions of Belgium, Finland, France,

Netherlands, Italy, Yugoslavia, Austria, Portugal, Switzerland, Spain, and Germany.

Southern Baptists have long used some international approaches in dealing with Europe. In the 1920s, Everett Gill, Sr., became superintendent of new Southern Baptist missions in Europe. After World War II, Southern Baptists sent Dr. Jesse D. Franks to serve as its relief coordinator throughout Europe. He often joined with representatives of other Baptist groups in giving help for relief and rehabilitation where it was needed. This work was continued by George W. Sadler and Josef Nordenhaug. As already noted, John Allen Moore became Southern Baptists' fraternal representative to the Baptists of eastern Europe and a bit later also the Foreign Mission Board's field representative for Europe. This made him a colleague and counselor of missionaries throughout Europe and of the Board's secretary for Europe and the Middle East. He was also the representative of the Foreign Mission Board to the European Baptist Federation and to Baptist groups where missionaries are not stationed. Isam Ballenger succeeded him as field representative for Europe and John David Hopper as fraternal representative to the Baptists of eastern Europe. When Ballenger became area director for Europe and the Middle East, Keith Parker was made his associate for Europe.

The Dream of an International Seminary

In 1908, at the first European Baptist Conference, a resolution voiced the hope for "an international Baptist university college at a central place." The only Baptist seminaries in Europe at that time were nine in Great Britain and Ireland, one in Sweden, and one in Germany.

At about the same time, some farseeing people on the other side of the Atlantic were thinking along similar lines. W. O. Carver, professor at The Southern Baptist Theological

Seminary, wrote to George W. Sadler in 1948:

> More than forty years ago Everett Gill and I discussed much the desirability that Baptists have a European center in Zurich. . . . We were thinking about this as a center for the dissemination of Baptist concepts of freedom in religion and in all ecclesiastical matters. That early base of our Anabaptist forebears holds geographical and cultural relations to the whole of Europe not matched by any other point, not even Geneva, certainly so far as our message and mission are concerned.

Enthusiasm for an international Baptist seminary in Europe reached a high peak in the Baptist World Congress of 1911. Delegates were deeply moved by accounts of the difficulties and heroism of Russian Baptists and by seeing a number of them in the Congress. The Russian Baptist prisoner, Pavloff, spoke on the Christianization of his land. He said, "We must have a college for education of our preachers, but under the present conditions it is not possible to establish it in our own country." A. J. Vining of Canada gave an impassioned address on "A Baptist Training School for Europe," in which he said:

> They plead, these patient veterans of Jesus Christ, for millions who wait for the coming of the trained evangelist and the pastor who is "apt to teach." Must these men call in vain? Shall we not gladly answer their appeal? There is one way in which their pleadings may be answered—a way in which every man here may make himself heard. Establish a great cosmopolitan Theological Seminary in the heart of Europe! Make it possible for the young Baptist men of the different countries of Europe to receive training that will qualify them to take the continent for Him who is worthy "to receive glory and honor and power." Give the peoples, whose representatives these men are, a training school, in which young Baptist ministers may receive help that will fit them for leadership, and in this hall are hundreds who will live to see Europe a great Protestant, Christian continent,

and Russia the mightiest Baptist stronghold on earth. . . .

Men of the North, men of the South, men of the East and men of the West, kindle a fire of hope on every mountain-peak in Europe today! Send the good news to millions of waiting, watching people, that we have this day decided to establish without delay a training school for the Baptists of Europe.

The chairman of the Congress announced that a delegation would be sent by the Baptist World Alliance to Russia to negotiate for the establishment of a Baptist university there. Pledges of gifts to start the school were then and there received. In a short time $66,000 had been promised. Further pledges were given before the Congress was over.

At a later session of the 1911 Congress, a committee of the Southern Baptist Convention presented a plan for the establishment of a Baptist seminary "specially for the training of Baptist pastors and evangelists in southern and southeastern Europe." Funds would be furnished mainly by Southern Baptists and Northern Baptists, and property would be held by trustees appointed by these two Conventions, but contributions by British and Canadian Baptists were foreseen. The school would be managed by a committee of Americans and British, appointed by the trustees.

Conditions in Russia at the time, followed by World War I, made impossible the establishment of the seminary as planned. By the time the executive committee of the Alliance and other representative Baptists met in London in 1920, the enthusiasm for an international seminary apparently had been lost. However, the importance of theological education was fully recognized. The following resolution was passed: "We regard an educational policy as of primary importance for the extension of the Baptist denomination in Europe, and we consider that the establishment or strengthening of Baptist seminaries for the training of pastors and evangelists should be undertaken without delay." Interesting also is the opinion expressed that Baptist seminaries "should be established, where possible, in the neighborhood of universities."

Establishment of the Ruschlikon Seminary

The idea of an international seminary seems to have lain dormant until the time of World War II. Its revival and implementation are to be credited mainly to George W. Sadler, at that time secretary for Africa, Europe, and the Near East of the Southern Baptist Foreign Mission Board. Influenced little, if at all, by previous thinking along this line, he and other Southern Baptists, notably M. Theron Rankin, general secretary of the Board, began to think and talk of a school where men from many different European countries could be trained for the ministry. This would be a significant contribution to the evangelization of Europe, the strengthening of the Baptist denomination, and the achievement of international understanding and world peace.

When the war ended, action was taken to make the dream of an international seminary come true. In April, 1948, the Southern Baptist Foreign Mission Board endorsed Dr. Sadler's recommendation for "the establishment of a Baptist theological seminary of graduate level in Europe, probably at Geneva."

When, in the 1948 European Conference in London called by the Baptist World Alliance to consider postwar strategy, Southern Baptists announced their intention to establish a seminary in Switzerland, strong opposition was expressed. Many people thought that if an international seminary were established, it should be under the auspices of the Baptist World Alliance or at least of an international committee. They were suspicious of the motives and distrustful of the ability of Southern Baptists. However, Dr. Sadler announced firmly but courteously that Southern

Baptists had decided to establish the seminary and would carry out their plans.

The Conference then adopted the report of its committee on theological education, (chaired by an Englishman, as the plural verbs with *committee* indicate), which included the following:

> The Committee stress the need for seminaries where national groups can teach their ministers in the languages in which they will preach the Gospel to their people and with special reference to the problems of their own nation.
>
> It was agreed, however, that beside these, and in no way replacing them, there is need of a seminary in Europe which shall be more than a national institution, a seminary which may satisfy the educational needs of several countries and which may be more of a graduate school than some of the smaller seminaries.
>
> The Committee recognize with gratitude the generosity of the brothers of the Southern Baptist Convention of the United States in their plans to establish a seminary in Switzerland which will serve wider than national interests.

It is rather generally recognized now that the seminary would not have come into being if one Baptist group had not taken the responsibility for it. Because of their numbers, Southern Baptists were better able than any other body to make the kind of investment that was called for. In the first Ruschlikon trustees' meeting (1950), Dr. Sadler said:

> It might seem impertinent for one Baptist group to decide to establish an institution of this sort in a distant land, but we knew that such an institution was needed, and decided to go ahead. We hope that you do not think that we were unduly impertinent or presumptuous. We certainly have no selfish ends to serve. We have no desire to supplant any other seminary. There should be ample evidence of this in the gifts that have been made to the seminaries in Oslo, Hamburg, Rivoli, and Holland, the support given to the seminaries in the Balkans and in Hungary, and the small amount contributed to repair the cloisters of Spurgeon's College. We are not

thinking in terms of supplanting but of supplementing the educational efforts of this continent.

The decision in the 1948 London Conference that any national Baptist organization should be "free to co-operate with any other Baptist bodies or mission boards within the fellowship of the Baptist World Alliance," with the understanding that there would be consultation and cooperation to avoid duplication or neglect, opened up the possibility of a more thoroughly international institution than was at first envisaged by Southern Baptists. They had originally thought that students would come mainly from those countries of southern and eastern Europe for which the Southern Baptist Convention had been given responsibility in 1920.

Not long after the London meeting, seminary property in Ruschlikon (Zurich), Switzerland, was purchased. Other sites in the Geneva and Zurich areas were considered, but none seemed nearly so adequate as the Bodmer estate, with its forty-room mansion. The purchase price was approximately $240,000.

Why was Switzerland chosen as the site of the seminary? Certainly not because it was a Baptist stronghold. There have been Baptists in Switzerland since the 1840s, mainly as a result of German influence, but churches in the Swiss Baptist Union had only about 1,300 members when the seminary was founded, and only 1,425 thirty years later. The only strong church was the one in Zurich. Not until several years after the establishment of the seminary was a bilingual church established in Lugano, and not until the 1960s was work among Italians in Switzerland begun. French-speaking Swiss Baptists, few in number, were too ultraconservative to participate in the Baptist World Alliance or the European Baptist Federation.

The seminary was established in Switzerland because

there it had the best chance of becoming international. In Italy it inevitably would have become Italian; in Germany it would have become German. The atmosphere of Switzerland nourishes internationalism.

One of the most significant developments was the formation of a board of trustees made up of Baptists from many different European countries. That most Baptist unions chose men well qualified in education or denominational administration indicated that European Baptists took seriously the new venture in Ruschlikon. Since the trustees were not responsible for raising funds, their functions were different from those of most trustees. Their duties as outlined in the first trustees' meeting were as follows: to act as a liaison between the seminary and national Baptist groups, to select students who would profit from study in Ruschlikon, to advise the seminary concerning needs in the various countries and ways in which the Ruschlikon center might help to meet those needs, to help correlate the different school systems and set up standards for admission, and to serve on advisory committees.

The seminary began its first session in September, 1949, under the leadership of Dr. Sadler, who had agreed to serve as acting president during the first year. The faculty included John D. W. Watts and John Allen Moore, Southern Baptist missionaries, and an Englishman, Arthur B. Crabtree. Claus Meister of Switzerland was engaged to teach in a preparatory department. Jesse D. Franks was administration secretary, treasurer, and chairman of public relations. Twenty-eight students (including two Methodists) of sixteen nationalities were enrolled during the first session.

Speaking of what the seminary ought to become, Dr. Sadler declared to the trustees in March, 1950:

> We do not believe that there is any conflict between Christianity and sound scholarship. We do not want to be

high-brow, but we do want to offer the best in Christ-centered education and scholarship.

We are now thinking in terms of offering a Bachelor of Divinity degree. All three of the Southern Baptist seminaries in America have agreed to recognize and give full credit for all courses and work completed here.

More Than Three Decades of Service

In 1950 Josef Nordenhaug was elected president of the Ruschlikon seminary. His Norwegian birth and education, his training at The Southern Baptist Theological Seminary, his editorship of the magazine published by the Foreign Mission Board, his linguistic ability, and his American citizenship qualified him well for the leadership of the international seminary. After serving ten years, Dr. Nordenhaug left Ruschlikon to become general secretary of the Baptist World Alliance.

In 1960 J. D. Hughey assumed the presidency. He had been a missionary in Spain before joining the Ruschlikon faculty. When he resigned in 1964 to become secretary for Europe and the Middle East of the Foreign Mission Board, John D. W. Watts, a member of the seminary faculty since the beginning and recognized all over Europe as a first-rate Old Testament scholar, succeeded him. When Watts resigned in 1970, John Allen Moore became the interim seminary president for a year. In the summer of 1971, Penrose St. Amant, former dean of The Southern Baptist Theological Seminary, became the president-elect. Faculty members rotated as faculty chairmen until St. Amant moved to Switzerland in 1972.

Dr. Isam Ballenger succeeded Dr. St. Amant as seminary president in 1977, and he continued to function also as field representative (or associate to the area director) for Europe. In September, 1980, Dr. Ronald Goulding became interim president of the seminary. He was the first European to direct the institution.

In 1982 Dr. Clyde Fant, a prominent American pastor and former professor at Southwestern Baptist Theological Seminary, accepted the presidency of the Ruschlikon seminary. He was nominated by the executive board of the seminary and elected by the European Baptist Federation Council and the Southern Baptist Foreign Mission Board. Dr. and Mrs. Fant were employed as missionary associates.

The late 1970s were years of financial pressure and uncertainty for the seminary, especially because of the decline of the value of the dollar in Switzerland. The Foreign Mission Board declared a limit on the subsidy it could provide, and it called on European Baptists to make up the difference. It offered the seminary property and sponsorship of the seminary to the European Baptist Federation Council for a period of five years. The offer was accepted, and control of the seminary passed to an executive board chosen by the European Baptist Federation Council and the Foreign Mission Board.

The financial picture soon improved, and the permanence of the seminary seemed assured. When Dr. Fant was elected president, the Foreign Mission Board renewed for ten years its agreements with the European Baptist Federation Council concerning the seminary.

Building a strong faculty has been a major concern through the years. The seminary has not been in a position to compete with great universities and seminaries so far as salaries are concerned, since the salary scale is the same as that of foreign missionaries; yet its faculty members are expected to operate on the academic level of faculty in those institutions. Furthermore, Ruschlikon has not offered the challenge of dealing with large numbers of students. However, some unusually competent persons have appreciated and accepted the opportunity of teaching there. In 1982 the faculty consisted of two Americans, three Germans, and one Swiss. Part-time lecturers and, from time to time, distinguished guest professors help bear the teaching load.

Through the years the curriculum has experienced significant developments, but always in the direction originally foreseen. After two years the preparatory department was abolished, since it seemed that students could best do their preuniversity or preseminary work in their own countries. A four-year Bachelor of Divinity (B.D.) course became the heart of the curriculum. This is open only to those who are eligible for study in university theological faculties in their own countries. However, the seminary has always accepted students who do not meet university entrance requirements. Since 1957, a research degree (Th.M.) calling for at least one year beyond the B.D. has been offered. The trend is clearly toward concentration on more advanced study than is possible in most of the national Baptist seminaries.

From the beginning, the value of a good relationship with the University of Zurich has been recognized. The university theological faculty grants B.D. honor graduates of the seminary a reduction in the number of fields on which they are examined for a doctorate. It also accepts Latin, Greek, and Hebrew certificates from the seminary as evidence that university language requirements have been met. Several Ruschlikon graduates have earned doctorates at the university.

Much progress has been made in buildings and equipment. An addition to the main building houses the best Baptist theological library and probably the best collection of theological books and periodicals in English to be found anywhere in Europe outside England. Buildings that have been constructed since the property was purchased include a student dormitory, two apartment buildings for married students, a house for the president, several faculty homes off campus, and a chapel building.

Buildings, equipment, curriculum, and faculty exist mainly for the sake of students. From the standpoint of numbers of students and what they have received, has the seminary proved worthwhile? Without doubt, the answer should be affirmative, although the enrollment has never exceeded seventy-four, the record reached in the 1982-83 session.

Since the number of Baptist seminaries on the continent of Europe, not counting those in Great Britain, has increased from two to fourteen during this century, the majority of ministerial students can study in their own countries. The few who go to Ruschlikon do so for more advanced study than they can do at home and/or for the broadening experience of study and fellowship in an international environment. The student body usually includes a few non-Europeans.

Ruschlikon alumni are serving as pastors, teachers, editors, denominational officers, and youth leaders in Europe and in several other continents as well. A number are foreign missionaries. More than a third of the program personalities at European Baptist conferences are usually Ruschlikon seminary alumni.

Theo van der Laan, a 1959 graduate of the Ruschlikon seminary, is a teacher in the Dutch Baptist Seminary. Formerly general secretary of the Baptist Union in the Netherlands, he has held pastorates in his own country and for three years was registrar and assistant to the Ruschlikon seminary president. He says his best memory of Ruschlikon is the miracle of a change in attitudes and the development of lasting friendship that followed a quarrel between him and a German student while memories of World War II were fresh. The German, who could not go to the mission field as he had planned, has become a prominent psychiatrist and an active church member.

Max and Susi Stäubli of Switzerland entered an open door for foreign missionary service in Africa following study at Ruschlikon for three years ending in 1962. They became missionaries of the European Baptist Mission, and he now serves that society in an administrative position.

José Borras, who received a B.D. degree from Ruschlikon in 1959 after having studied also at the Baptist seminary in Spain, is director of the latter seminary. Formerly a Roman Catholic priest, his quest for spiritual vitality led him to conversations with Baptists in the town where he taught in a Catholic school and eventually to membership in a Spanish Baptist church. He met his future wife, the daughter of a Baptist pastor. She was the first Spanish Baptist woman to receive a university degree. She joined her husband in Ruschlikon for three semesters of seminary study. Borras has held pastorates in Spain and is in great demand as a preacher. He has participated in evangelistic campaigns in America, Puerto Rico, Lebanon, the Philippines, Holland, Austria, Portugal, and elsewhere. He has served with distinction as president of the Spanish Baptist Union. He said:

> I believe the seminary of Ruschlikon is a great blessing for European Baptists. Although most of the subjects that are taught in this seminary can be taught also in the national seminaries, there are certain things that can be received only in an international seminary, such as the international atmosphere, the interchange of ideas and traditions, and the acquaintance with future leaders of Baptist work in other countries.

Only a few of the graduates of the Ruschlikon seminary have been mentioned. They are reminders that the influence of such a school reaches far and goes deep.

Nonacademic Functions at Ruschlikon

Almost from the beginning of the seminary, summer conferences have been a regular feature of the Ruschlikon program. European Baptists needed a place where they could get acquainted with one another, learn from one another and from conference leaders, and make plans for the future. The facilities were available and, since kitchen and household personnel had to be employed on an annual basis, hospitality could be offered European guests without great extra expense.

At first, conference programs were prepared by members of the Ruschlikon center staff, and some continue to be. More and more, however, groups or committees within the European Baptist Federation have taken over this responsibility.

Among those for whom conferences have been arranged in Ruschlikon, some for several times, are the following: pastors, laymen, women, young people, missionary leaders, Sunday School workers, church musicians, theological teachers, writers, public-school teachers, physicians, persons interested in broadcasting, leaders in evangelism and religious education, and presidents and secretaries of Baptist unions. All have had their horizons extended, gained new insights, and established international friendships.

A conference of editors and publishers at Ruschlikon several years ago sensed and expressed the need for the regular sharing of news among European Baptists and also for informing others of significant developments among Baptists. The Foreign Mission Board responded to the appeal for assistance in this worthy project by permitting a missionary to give half time to a "European Baptist Press Service" and later by assigning a missionary to work full time with it.

A conference of persons interested in broadcasting resulted in the establishment of a radio recording studio at Ruschlikon (inaugurated in 1964). Though owned and operated by the Southern Baptist Foreign Mission Board, the studio has the approval and guidance of the European Baptist Federation. Programs for broadcasting in many languages—including Hungarian, Russian, Italian, Spanish, Portuguese, and French—have been prepared wholly or partially in Ruschlikon. The production of most programs has shifted to the countries that use the languages.

Many of the programs are over a shortwave religious broadcasting station, since outlets in Europe are limited by state ownership of most radio and television stations. Wesley Miller, director of the studio, has said, "Short-wave radio is essentially international in character. In places like eastern Europe, particularly, one cannot broadcast on the local radio or television stations except on rare occasions. To hear anything but the government line, listeners turn to short-waves where they can receive signals from many other countries and compare the stories they hear. That is a ready audience, too, for the religious broadcaster."

In 1967 Miller became the Foreign Mission Board's radio and television representative for Europe and the Middle East. He counsels missionaries and nationals of many countries about broadcasting, cultivates relationships with broadcasters, plans and participates in conferences and broadcasting workshops, and teaches occasional courses in the Ruschlikon seminary.

For several years a Summer Institute for Theological Education (SITE) has been held in Ruschlikon. Young pastors and others from eastern Europe find it much easier to get away from their own countries for four or five weeks than for a semester or year. Each is given a "mini library" to take home with him—in most cases more books than he has ever dreamed of having. Though eastern Europeans are given preference, students from other countries are also accepted. Funds for SITE are raised independently of the seminary budget, mainly from European sources.

Ruschlikon has become a Baptist center for Europe. It is a meeting place of languages, cultures, and traditions, and a laboratory where men and women can discover how their oneness in Christ overshadows all differences. Partly because of it, European Baptists know one another better and have more ways of cooperating than do the Baptists of any other continent.

Several years ago a taxi driver who had taken several people from the Ruschlikon train station to the seminary for a conference said: "You have people coming here from everywhere, and they all seem to be friends." Would it not be wonderful for the whole world to be like that? Perhaps in a small way those who go to Ruschlikon are helping to make the world a friendlier place in which to live.

International Efforts in Evangelism

We have already noted that European Baptists as well as Southern Baptists have become aware of the need of service and evangelism among the five or six million Muslims living in Western Europe. German Baptists have requested a Southern Baptist missionary couple to help them in an outreach to Muslims. In 1982 a converted Muslim from Iran sent to Germany by the Foreign Mission Board helped Germans and Americans develop a ministry to Muslims.

Missionaries and Belgian Baptists are considering the development of a Baptist center in Brussels to expand the present English-language ministry to French, Flemish, Spanish, and Arabic-speaking persons. In various countries Muslims have already been enlisted in Bible study and worship, and a few have made professions of faith in Christ.

Partnership evangelism campaigns have been conducted

with considerable success in various European countries. The partnerships now include Baptists of other European countries as well as Americans. It is hoped that more and more churches in America will arrange for teams from Europe to help them.

The international approach in missions is appreciated overseas because it meets needs without interfering with the autonomy that is essential for the development of Baptist churches and conventions. It does not take the place of missionary efforts centered on particular countries but supplements and enriches them.

Baptist experiments in internationalism are part of the response to Europe as a mission field. European Baptists cannot escape their mission responsibility, nor can Southern Baptists. The Baptists (and other Christians) of some countries must stand almost alone—yet not alone, for God is with them, and they are not forgotten by their brothers and sisters in Christ of other lands. Sometimes help can go from one country to another, or from one country to many. Sometimes a truly international effort can be made. All are important.

7/"A Policy of Reliable Partnership"

The title of this chapter is the same as the title of an article in the 1981 spring issue of *Foreign Affairs* by Helmut Schmidt, chancellor of the Federal Republic of Germany. He emphasizes the helpful political partnership that has developed between Europeans, especially Germans, and Americans. Our focus is on international partnership in the gospel, especially as experienced in Europe. It is the kind of partnership that the apostle Paul and the Philippian Christians had with each other (Phil. 1:3-5).

Can our partners depend on us? Do we have a "reliable partnership"? Is this our fixed policy—something we have decided to do and will do regardless of circumstances? What are the requirements for a reliable partnership?

The first requirement is common interest or concern.

Nations become allies in order to defend themselves against a common enemy or to achieve mutually desirable goals such as the establishment or preservation of a particular form of government or social order. Businessmen and women form partnerships with each other because they share interest in producing or marketing certain products and think they can do it together effectively and profitably. The apostle Paul and the Philippian Christians formed a partnership in the gospel because they had experienced personally the value of the gospel and wanted others to do the same.

The Southern Baptist Convention was organized in 1845 "for eliciting, combining and directing the energies of the denomination for the propagation of the gospel." Missionary concern created the denomination, and this same concern has held us together.

Our partners in Europe share our concern for evangelizing Europe. Perhaps their concern exceeds our own. They know firsthand that Europeans need the gospel and that much depends on whether Baptists offer it to them. They know the value of churches and other institutions that offer vital Christian faith and the Christian way of life to those who have grown up with only secondhand or thirdhand contact with Christianity.

Dr. Gerhard Claas, general secretary of the Baptist World Alliance, tells of an old lady in Moscow who set for herself the goal of winning one person to Christ each month. Near the end of the year she said to her pastor, "I have failed. I have led only seven people to Christ this year." Dr. Claas exclaimed, "Where are my seven?"

How concerned are we for the eight hundred million Muslims of the world—and for the six million in western Europe? Does it matter to us that many people in Europe have the form but not the substance of Christianity? Are we concerned about Europe's drift away from God? How do we show our concern? If we are really interested, we can stand beside and work with missionaries and national Christians who are truly interested and much concerned.

A second essential for reliable partnership is mutual respect and confidence.

This is certainly true for a partnership between nations or for a business or professional partnership. It is dangerous for nations that are allies to lose confidence in each other. It is tragic for a person to doubt, or have reason to doubt, the honesty, integrity, or ability of his business or professional partner.

The Philippian Christians trusted and respected Paul. He trusted and respected them. He wrote them, "I am sure that he who began a good work in you will bring it to completion" (1:6, RSV).

During my thirty-eight years of working with missionaries, I developed great respect for them. With a few rare exceptions—fewer than in any other group I know—they are genuine in their faith, earnest in their Christian witness, honorable in their conduct, and far above average in ability and dedication.

Can missionaries have confidence in us? Can they be sure of our well-informed prayer support? Will Southern Baptists continue their financial support, not just of missionaries but also of the work which they and their national colleagues are doing? Will those in fruitful fields where expansion is possible be upheld with prayer and money? What about those who have been called to difficult places and sometimes cry out, "How long, O Lord?" Some of the most faithful, and most successful, missionaries are those who work for years without being able to tell many so-called "success stories."

What about our fellow Baptists in other countries? Can we have confidence in them? Yes, with remarkably few exceptions. I have been impressed with the ability, integrity, and Christian dedication of European Baptist leaders. Years ago a Baptist leader in Hungary threw his arms around me as I was leaving his country and said, "Please believe in us." I said, "I do, and I will." I have done so and still do.

Recent disputes in the Southern Baptist Convention imperil our partnership with Baptists of other countries. Can our partners in Europe and in other continents continue to trust us and be confident of our trust in them and our readiness to treat them as real partners?

When respect and confidence are threatened, everything possible must be done to restore and strengthen them. We may need to examine ourselves, ask forgiveness, accept it, change attitudes, change procedures, and keep trying.

Not long ago the president of the Italian Baptist Union said, "Our relationships with the missionaries have never been better. We fight like brothers. We have always fought, but now we fight like brothers." Mutual frankness, respect, confidence, and love can and should grow.

A third requirement for a reliable partnership is receiving and giving on both sides.

National allies give to and receive from each other. America has rightly given of its abundance to other nations, but it has often been too proud to learn from them or otherwise to receive from them. Business partners invest time and money in a business, and they receive benefits from their investment. They help each other.

The apostle Paul gave much—time, energy, love, the gospel. He was willing to endure all kinds of hardships to share himself and the gospel with other people. However, he also received. He wrote to the Philippians:

> It was kind of you to share my trouble. And you Philippians yourselves know that in the beginning of the gospel, when I left Macedonia, no church entered into partnership with me in giving and receiving except you only; for even in Thessalonica you sent me help once and again. I have received full payment and more; I am filled, having received from Epaphroditus the gifts you sent, a fragrant offering, a sacrifice acceptable and pleasing to God (Phil. 4:14-16,18, RSV).

We need to learn how to receive from our partners in the gospel. It is harder than giving. Not long ago Peter Barber, the general secretary of the Baptist Union of Scotland, and I talked about partnership between Southern Baptists and Scottish Baptists. He spoke of help by Southern Baptists in evangelism, church planting, and counseling. Then he asked, "What can Scottish Baptists do for Southern Baptists?" We agreed that they have much to contribute in the areas of Bible teaching and biblical preaching. Yet we had trouble getting preaching engagements not long after that for Barber's associate, who spent a month in America. We are geared up better for giving than receiving.

We can learn from people everywhere. How we need to learn from the Baptists of Communist countries about faithfulness, endurance, flexibility, and the importance of baptism as a turning point in life. From those who work in relatively unresponsive areas, we can learn to rejoice over one sinner who repents. From people in many lands, we can learn the meaning of trust in the Lord.

Everybody needs to learn how to regard the helping hand, how to receive counsel, and how to accept money or other material help when such help is needed. It is important to receive with dignity and gratitude, without taking gifts for granted or becoming dependent on them, and without humiliation or apology.

However, giving is also essential—the giving of money, time, and life. All can give. One of the first Baptist churches in Spain to become financially independent was the one in Barceloneta. The people were poor, but they saved their money for the church during the week and made a real offering of love on Sunday. Jesus said, "It is more blessed to give than to receive" (Acts 20:35).

Giving should be done without pride or ostentation, without ulterior motives, without making giving an instrument towards power, without expecting gratitude or understanding; it should be with love, generosity, helpfulness, and wisdom.

God asks us not only to give our money but also to give

our lives to him, to do his will in whatever way he indicates. The will of God unfolds for most people in secular vocations, voluntary church work, generous giving, and personal Christian witnessing. However, he calls some to church-related vocations in America and still others to foreign missionary service. A foreign missionary is a person with a mission for Christ away from home.

During my freshman year in college, the Lord dealt in a special way with me, and I told him, "I'll be a preacher if that is what you want me to be." Early in my first pastorate after seminary graduation, my wife and I decided that God was speaking to us through the spiritual needs of war-torn and secularized Europe. In effect we said, "Here we are, Lord; send us to Europe if that is your will."

I am glad God has permitted me to serve for so many years in the mission cause. If I had my life to live over again, I would like for it to be different in several ways, but I would not want any changes in its basic course.

Regardless of where we are, we are or can be members of a wonderful partnership in the gospel. May God help us to follow "a policy of reliable partnership."

Appendix 1/Baptist Headquarters in Europe

European Baptist Federation:
Dr. Knud Wümpelmann, Secretary
Laerdalsgade 7
DK-2300 Copenhagen S, Denmark

European Baptist Convention (English Language):
Rev. John W. Merritt, Secretary
Sonnenberger Strasse 60
D-6200 Wiesbaden, W. Germany

Austria:
Dr. Helmut Rabenau, Secretary
Moerikeweg 16
A-1160 Vienna

Belgium:
Rev. Henri Bens, President
Rue Eugène Simons 16
B-4020 Liège

Bulgaria:
Rev. Iwan Angelov, President
Pelo Pelovsky 63
1303 Sofia

Czechoslovakia:
Rev. Stanislav Svec, Secretary
Na Topolce 10
Prague 4

Denmark:
Rev. Gunnar Kristensen, Secretary
Laerdalsgade 5
DK-2300 Copenhagen S

Finland (Finnish Speaking):
Rev. Jouko Neulanen, President
Etu-Kanavuori
40800 Vaajakoski

Finland (Swedish Speaking):
Rev. Rafael Edström, President
Raedhusgatan 44 A
SF-65100 Vasa 10

France:
Rev. André Thobois, President
123 avenue du Maine
F-75014 Paris

Germany—East:
Rev. Rolf Dammann, Secretary
Gubener Strasse 10/I
DDR-1034 Berlin

137

Germany—West:

Rev. Siegfried Kerstan, Secretary
Friedberger Strasse 101
6380 Bad Homburg v.d.H.

Great Britain:

Rev. Bernard Green, Secretary
4 Southampton Row
London WC1B 4AB

Hungary:

Rev. Janos Laczkovszki, President
Aradi Utca 48
Budapest VI

Italy:

Dr. Piero Bensi, President
Piazza S. Lorenzo in Lucina 35
1-00186 Rome

Netherlands:

Rev. Jan Brandsma, Secretary
Biltseweg 10
NL-3735 MC Bosch en Duin (Bilthoven)

Norway:

Rev. Per Midteide, Secretary
Micheletsvei 62
N-1320 Stabekk

Poland:

Rev. Michal Stankiewicz, Secretary
ul. Walicow 25
00-865 Warsaw

Portugal:

Rev. Luis Almeida, Secretary
Rua Goncalves Crespo, 33-3 Frente
1100 Lisbon 1

Rumania:

Rev. Pavel Barbetei, Secretary
Nicolai Titulescu 56/1
7815 Bucharest

Scotland:

Rev. Peter Barber, Secretary
14 Aytoun Road
Glasgow G41 5 RT

Spain:

Rev. Pedro Bonet, President
Ciudad de Balaguer 40
Barcelona 22

Sweden:

Dr. David Lagergren, Secretary
Nortullsgatan 10, 1
S-113 27 Stockholm

Switzerland:

Rev. Ernst Binder, President
Hintersteig 25, CH8200
Schaffhausen

USSR:

Rev. Alexei Bichkov, Secretary
Pokrousky Boulevard Malyi Vusovsky 3
Post Office Box 520
Moscow

Wales: Rev. D. I. Davies, Secretary
94 Mansel Street
Abertawe/Swansea SA1 5TU

Yugoslavia: Dr. Josip Horak, President
Kordunska 4/III
41000 Zagreb

Appendix 2/Southern Baptist Missionary Contact Persons (1982)

Updated information is available from Dr. Keith Parker, associate to the area director for Europe, Gheistrasse 31, 8803 Ruschlikon, Switzerland, or from the Foreign Mission Board of the Southern Baptist Convention, 3806 Monument Avenue, Richmond, Virginia 23230.

Austria: Mrs. Sandy Huneycutt
Girzenberggasse 20
A-1130 Vienna

Belgium: Rev. James Kirkendall
Avenue des Muguets 13
1150 Brussels

France: Rev. Hal B. Lee
Res. le Lac
2 bis rue des Anglais
91300 Massy (Paris)

Germany—West: Rev. Kenneth Glenn
Föhrenweg 11
8000 Munich 90

Greece: Rev. David Hause
30 Naypaktou
Ano Glyfada, Athens

Italy: Dr. Albert Craighead
Via Luigi Colla 22
10098 Rivoli (To)

Portugal: Rev. Harry Hampsher
Ave. Bombeiros Voluntarios
Lote 110-11-F (Alges)
1495 Lisbon

Scotland: Rev. Loren Turnage
                                   17 Stonehaven Road
                                   Aberdeen AB1 5 US
Spain: Rev. Larry Henry
                                   Edificio las Robinias
                                   Torre 1-4-1
                                   Almeria
Switzerland: Dr. Clyde Fant
                                   Gheistrasse 31
                                   8803 Ruschlikon

Appendix 3/Where Attend Church?

The times of Sunday morning services are given. Many churches also have Sunday evening services, Sunday School, and midweek services. Information about other places can be obtained from addresses in Appendices 1 and 2 and from the Foreign Mission Board of the Southern Baptist Convention, 3806 Monument Avenue, Richmond, Virginia 23230.

Austria
  Salzburg: Schumacher Strasse 18; 9:30 (German), 11:15 (English).
  Vienna: Mollardgasse 35; 9:30 (German), 11:30 (English).
Belgium
  Brussels: 17 rue Jacque Hoton; 11:00 (English).
  Jurbise: 21 rue des Princes; 11:00 (English).
Czechoslovakia
  Prague: Vinohradska 68; 9:00 (Czech).
Denmark
  Copenhagen: Baggesensgade 7; 9:30 (Danish).
England
  Bedford: Bunyan Meeting, Mill Street; 11:00 (English).
  Kettering: Fuller Memorial Baptist Church; 11:00 (English).
  London: Ealing, Haven Green; 11:00 (English).
              Bloomsbury, Shaftesbury Avenue off New Oxford Street; 11:00 (English).
              Metropolitan Tabernacle, Newington Butts; 11:00 (English).

Finland
    Turku: Vähä-Hämeenkatu 16; 12:00 (Finnish)
France
    Paris: 123 avenue du Maine; 10:30 (French).
        48 rue de Lille; 10:30 (French).
        86 rue des Bons Raisins; 10:00 (English).
Germany—East
    Berlin: Mattern Strasse 17; 9:30.
Germany—West
    Augsburg: Grimm Strasse 8; 9:30 (German), 12:30 P.M. (English).
    Berlin: Rothenburg Strasse 13; 9:30 (German), 11:30 (English).
    Frankfurt: Am Tiergarten 50; 9:30 (German).
                Am Dachsberg 92; 11:00 (English).
    Hamburg: Grindelallee 101; 10:00 (German).
    Heidelberg: Feuerbach Strasse 4; 9:30 (German), 11:25 (English).
    Kaiserslautern: Adolf-Kolping-Platz 14; 9:30 (German).
                    Lichtenbruecher Strasse 17; 11:00 (English).
    Munich: Holz Strasse 9; 9:30 (German), 12:45 P.M. (English).
    Wiesbaden: Friedrich-Naumann-Strasse 25; 9:30 (German), 11:00
                (English).
Greece
    Athens: 58 Vouliagmenis, Ano Hellinikon; 11:00 (English).
Hungary
    Budapest: Nap-utca 40; 10:00 (Hungarian).
Italy
    Florence: Borgo Ognissanti 6; 11:00 (Italian).
    Milan: Via Pinamonte da Vimercate 10; 10:30 (Italian).
    Naples: Via Foria 93; 11:00 (Italian).
            Via Piccolo, Parco Mazzola, Lago Patria; 11:00 (English).
    Rome: Via Teatro Valle 27; 11:00 (Italian).
            Via delle Spighe 8; 11:00 (Italian).
            Piazza San Lorenzo in Lucina 35; 10:00 (English).
Netherlands
    Amsterdam: Postjesweg 150; 10:30 (Dutch).
Norway
    Oslo: Hausmannsgata 22; 11:00 (Norwegian).
    Stavanger: Bergjelandsgata 24; 11:00 (Norwegian), 1:00 P.M. (English).
Poland
    Warsaw: ul. Walicow 25; 10:00 (Polish).
Portugal
    Lisbon: Rua Filipe Folque 36 B; 11:00 (Portuguese).
Rumania
    Bucharest: Nicolai 56A; 11:00 (Rumanian).

Scotland
    Aberdeen: Cults Primary School; 11:00 (English).
    Edinburgh: 18 Morningside Road; 11:00 (English)
    Glasgow: Queen's Drive; 11:00 (English).
Spain
    Barcelona: Ciudad de Balaguer 40; 12:00 (Spanish).
    Madrid: General Lacy 18; 12:00 (Spanish).
          Hernandez de Tejada 4; 11:00 (English).
Sweden
    Stockholm: Norrtullsgatan 37; 11:00 (Swedish).
Switzerland
    Ruschlikon: Gheistrasse 31; 9:30 (German), 7:30 PM (English).
    Zurich: Steinwies Strasse 34; 9:30 (German).
USSR
    Leningrad: Bolshaja Osjornaja 29 A at Poklonnaja Gora; 9:00 (Russian).
    Moscow: Pokrousky Boulevard Malyi Vusovsky 3; 9:00 (Russian).
Yugoslavia
    Belgrade: Branka Cretkovico 33; 9:30 (Serbo-Croation)
    Zagreb: Radicheva 30; 9:30 (Serbo-Croation)

Appendix 4/Some Places of Special Interest to Christian Tourists

Austria
    Vienna: St. Stephen's Cathedral
Denmark
    Copenhagen: Cathedral, with statues by Thorvaldsen
    Tølløse: Baptist Seminary and Folk High School
France
    Avignon: Palace of the Popes during the "Babylonian Captivity"
    Chartres: Cathedral
    Paris: Baptist Pastoral School and Mass Media Center (Massy)
          Church of the Madeleine
          Notre Dame Cathedral
          Sainte Chapelle
Germany—East
    Berlin: Baptist Book Store

Buckow: Baptist Seminary
Wartburg Castle, near Eisenach: Refuge of Luther
Wittenberg: Where Reformation began
Germany—West
  Aachen: Cathedral where Holy Roman Emperors were crowned
  Augsburg: Scene of the Augsburg Confession and the Peace of
          Augsburg
  Cologne: Cathedral
  Hamburg: Baptist Seminary
  Oberammergau: Passion Play
  Worms: Where Luther refused to recant; Reformation monument
Great Britain
  Bedford: Where Bunyan was imprisoned
  Canterbury: Cathedral
  Edinburgh: St. Giles Church, where John Knox preached
  Glasgow: Baptist Theological College
  Kettering: Where Baptist Missionary Society was organized
  London: Baptist Church House
        St. Paul's Church
        Spurgeon's College
        Westminster Abbey
Greece
  Athens: Mars Hill, near Acropolis
Italy
  Assisi: Home of St. Francis
  Florence: Cathedral
        Michelangelo's statue of David in the Academy Gallery
  Milan: Cathedral
      Leonardo da Vinci's Last Supper in Santa Maria delle Grazie˙
  Rivoli: Baptist Center, including Linguistic School
  Rome: Baptist Media Center
      Catacombs
      Cathedral of St. John in Lateran
      Church of St. Peter in Chains (statue of Moses by Michelangelo)
      Colosseum, where Christians were martyred
      Mammertine Prison
      St. Peter's Church (ancient statue of Peter and Michelangelo's
        Pieta)
      Vatican Palace (Sistine Chapel)
  Turin: Cathedral, which houses the reputed Holy Shroud
  Venice: Basilica of St. Mark

Netherlands
  Amsterdam: City which was temporary home of the first English
           Baptists
  Bosch en Duin (Bilthoven): Baptist Seminary
Norway
  Stabekk: Baptist Seminary
Poland
  Warsaw: Baptist Seminary
Portugal
  Lisbon: Jeronimos Church
        Baptist Book Store
  Lisbon (Que Luz): Baptist Seminary
Spain
  Barcelona: Baptist Book Store
          Cathedral
          Church of the Holy Family
  Denia: Baptist Camp and Conference Center
  El Escorial: Monastery built by Philip II
  Madrid (Alcobendas): Baptist Seminary
  Madrid: Plaza Mayor, scene of autos de fe
  Montserrat: Monastery
  Toledo: Cathedral
       Synagogue
Sweden
  Bromma, near Stockholm: Baptist Seminary
Switzerland
  Geneva: Reformation Monument
         St. Peter's Church, where Calvin preached
  Ruschlikon: Baptist Theological Seminary
  Zurich: Fraumünster (Women's Church), once part of a convent
        Grossmünster (Big Church), where Zwingli preached
        Wasserkirche (Water Church) and statue of Zwingli
        Sites related to the Anabaptist movement
Turkey
  Istanbul: Blue Mosque
        St. Sophia, built by Justinian as a church, later made a
          mosque, now a museum
Yugoslavia
  Novi Sad: Baptist Seminary